Rough Notes of a Trip to
REUNION

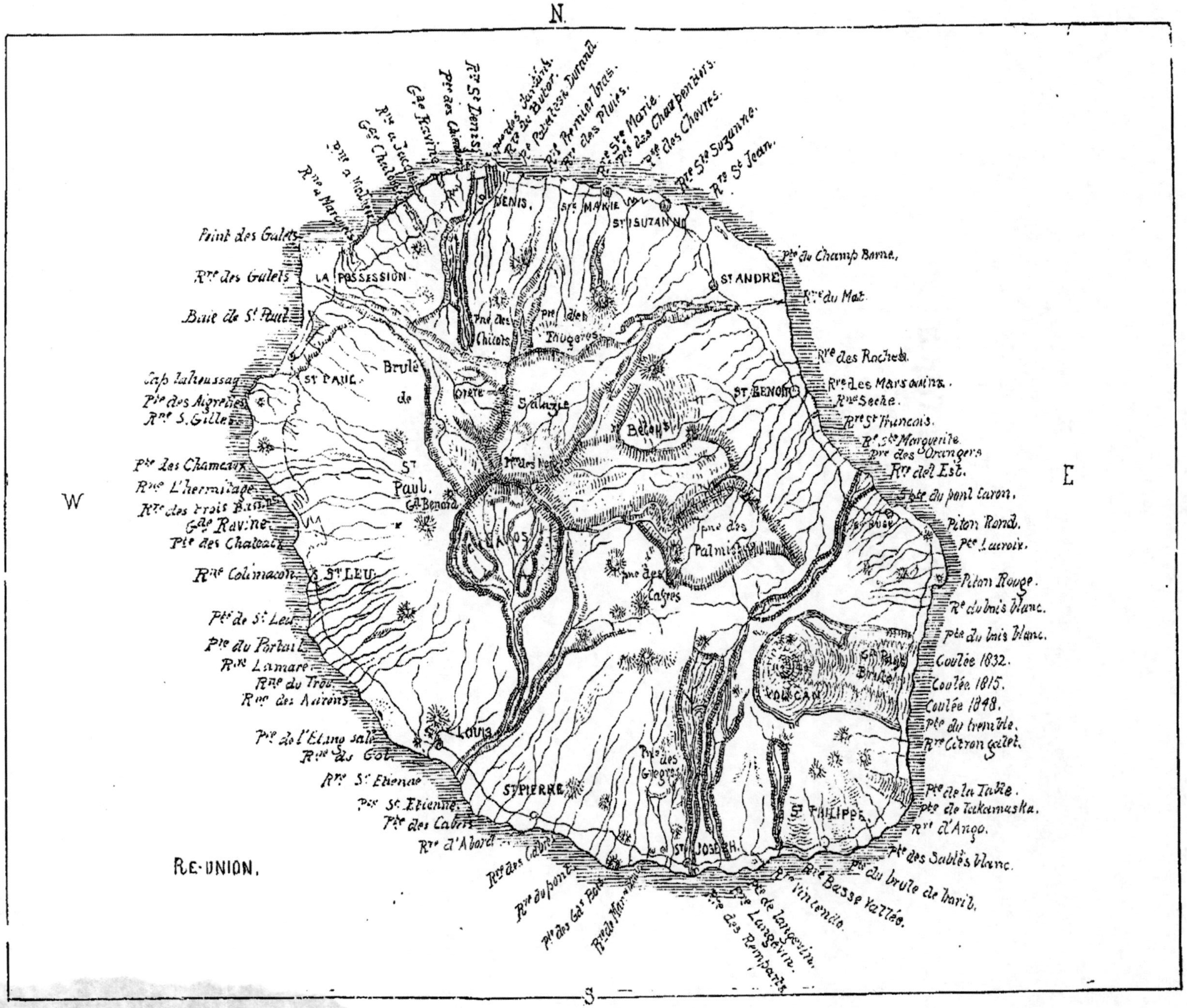

N
E
S
W
RE-UNION.
St DENIS
Ste MARIE
Ste SUZANNE
St ANDRE
St BENOIT
LA POSSESSION
St PAUL
St LEU
St LOUIS
St PIERRE
St JOSEPH
St PHILIPPE
VOLCAN
Salazie
Belouve
Cilaos
Brulé de St Paul
Point des Galets
Baie de St Paul
Cap Lahoussaye
Piton Rond
Piton Rouge
Coulée 1832.
Coulée 1815.
Coulée 1848.

Rough Notes of a Trip to
REUNION

MAURITIUS
and
CEYLON

Frederic J. Mouat M. D.

ISBN : 978-93-5324-567-2 (HB)
First Published, 1852
Published, 2020
Published by
Facsimile Publisher
12 Pragati Market
Ashok Vihar, Ph-2
Delhi-110052
E-mail: books@facsimilepublisher.com
Printed at: G. Print Process, Delhi.

Rough Notes of a Tip to Reunion
Mauritius and Ceylon
Author: Frederic J. Mouat M. D.

PREFACE.

In December of 1850 sudden and severe sickness compelled me to seek temporary change, with relaxation from duty, after a nearly unbroken residence in Lower Bengal of more than ten years. I was somewhat embarrassed as to the direction in which it would be most advisable to search for complete restoration in the shortest space of time.

My personal predilections were in favour of the islands in the southern part of the Indian Ocean; but on enquiry I found it extremely difficult to procure any information to guide me in the selection of a Sanitarium.

Others may possibly experience the same difficulty, and as I not only regained health and strength, but derived a considerable amount of pleasure and amusement from my trip, I have ventured to publish a portion of my notes for the information of those similarly circumstanced.

It is not, I believe, generally known that there exists in the little island of Bourbon, within a few days' sail of Calcutta, one of the finest and most healthy climates in the whole world, grand and beautiful scenery, and mineral waters of rare virtue and efficacy.

The Mauritius, being a British colonial possession carrying on an extended intercourse with India, is much better known, but comparatively few are aware of its great advantages as a resort for Indian Invalids.

The hill districts of Ceylon, on the very threshold of Hindustan, are easily and constantly accessible, and frequently visited by pilgrims in search of health. They possess many advantages to recommend them to notice in a sanitary point of view, yet it is surprizing how very vague and imperfect is the information to be gathered in India regarding them.

My notes are exactly what they profess to be, rough and unpolished. They pretend to no literary excellence, attempt no researches into the arcana of science in any of its departments, and are simply intended to guide others in the path that proved eminently beneficial to myself.

The illustrations are executed by Mr. C. Grant, chiefly from drawings published in the Mauritius and Bourbon, which I brought up with me.

They convey a very faithful image of the places they are intended to represent, and will, I believe, be deemed a favourable evidence of the gradual progress of art "under difficulties" in the East, where Lithography is a compulsory, as it is also a novel substitute for Wood Engraving, and so little has been heretofore attempted in a direction now pursued with such success in Europe.

ILLUSTRATIONS.

A
TRIP TO REUNION.

ROUGH NOTES OF A TRIP TO RE-UNION.

THE PASSAGE.

At four in the afternoon of Friday, the 25th of April, 1851, whilst amusing myself at the window of my excellent and facetious friend C—— of Port Louis, watching the pretty girls passing the corner of the Place D'Armes—and they are neither few nor far between—there suddenly arose a stir and bustle near the news room. A small quadrangular notice was being rapidly posted and pasted on every available spot for public advertisements, and around them were soon assembled groups of curious spectators. We had for some time contemplated a trip to the neighbouring island of Re-union, and had formed a small party for the excursion, but no means of getting there had up to that time been available.

A French ship, the Admiral Duperré of Bordeaux, was to start at the beginning of the succeeding week, and the gallant little war schooner, the Eglé, was also to wend her way across, as soon as the European mail arrived: upon the first of these that started we had resolved to trust our fortunes.

At the moment of posting the notice referred to, I had in my hand a Dolland's telescope of which I had just become the fortunate possessor, testing its virtues upon the countenances of the fair passers by. It was forthwith directed to the mysterious paper, when it brought distinctly to view the following—

"PUBLIC NOTICE."

"THE GOVERNMENT STEAMER 'PRINCE ALBERT' WILL BE DESPATCHED TO RE-UNION, TO-MORROW, SATURDAY, THE 26TH INST. AT 4 P. M. FOR FREIGHT OR PASSAGE APPLY TO

Port Louis, April 25, 1851. HUNTER, IRELAND AND CO."

An involuntary shout of, Hurrah for Bourbon! brought forth the other inmates of C.'s hospitable house, viz., himself and our proposed fellow-traveller, a gallant son of Mars, owning Madras as his presidency, and holding a responsible appointment in the commission ruled over by one of the most amiable, excellent, and gifted officers in the whole of British India.

We incontinently held a committee of ways and means, and resolved, wind, weather, and the non-arrival of the mail permitting, to honour His Royal Highness with our society to the roadstead of St. Denis.

In this mood of mind each made his preparations for the coming event, but the dawn of the succeeding morning somewhat deranged our well-devised plan. The flag-staff of the adjoining signal station presented at the mast-head a mysterious black ball, which, on being interpreted, notified the advent of the mail schooner from Point de Galle. Calms, contrary winds, and the like catalogue of drawbacks to which those who *sail* in ships are subject, had delayed her some days beyond the expected and usual time of transit. The additional life, animation, and bustle infused into the already busy, cheerful, and stirring community of Port Louis by her arrival, were pleasing to witness, and strong proofs of the energy and spirit of its mixed population. Indeed, I have never seen a town of similar dimensions, with so much of the genuine elements of the great business of life, or exhibiting on so small a scale so large an amount of healthy activity. Although a latent spirit of the old French and English antagonism is deeply grafted in its constitution, and occasionally exhibits itself in an unseemly brawl, or an ominous growl; yet does it appear, on the whole, to be a thriving, prosperous, and tolerably united settlement. One is apt to wonder where the numerous shops that crowd its well-peopled streets, can possibly find customers to dispose of their multifarious, and, in general, extremely dear wares. Its well-regulated, clean and inodorous market-place is by far the best thing of the kind in the

east, and a striking contrast to the dirty, noisy, ill-regulated bazars of Calcutta. The plentiful supply of sparkling wholesome water, distributed in every direction through neat and tasteful fountains; the order, decorum, and cleanliness of the rectangular streets; the number of well-dressed, good-looking ladies perambulating its busy thoroughfares; and the stand of carriages for hire in front of the Government House, some of them with no mean pretensions to elegance, strike the visitor from India as something more suggestive of home, and pleasing, than even the imposing wealth of the city of palaces, the fine roads and park-like compounds of Madras, or the pretty and picturesque appearance of the well-watered capital of Ceylon, with its cinnamon gardens, lakes, and islands!

By an amicable arrangement with the English government, and the existence of the friendly feeling which every real well-wisher to his country is rejoiced to witness between France and Great Britain, the mail intended for Bourbon, and the French settlements in Madagascar, is carried to Galle by the Peninsular and Oriental Company's steamers. It is thence transmitted to the Mauritius, in a separate box, on the Government mail schooners of that island. To transport it to its ultimate destination is the special duty of a beautiful little war schooner, the Églé, commanded by M. Leclair, an officer in the republican navy. She invariably starts in the afternoon of the day of arrival of the European mail, and usually carries down those desirous of making the acquaintance of the sister isle. My friends had made arrangements to go down in her, while I was induced by private and personal considerations to prefer the steamer—this caused our temporary separation.

After paying twenty dollars for my passage, and completing the few arrangements left unfinished, both parties embarked at four in the afternoon of a heavenly day, with a fine fresh favourable breeze blowing—the Églé weighing anchor and standing out about half an hour sooner than the Prince Albert.

There are probably few prettier and more picturesque sights in the world than the sea-board view of the Mauritius on a fine clear day. The forts,

churches, and harbour of Port Louis, with the singular hills under the lee of which it lies imbedded, of themselves form a strikingly interesting picture. The curious, almost grotesque appearance of the far-famed Peter Botte, with the bold sweep of the Pouce, terminating in an abrupt bluff of rock on which stands the signal station, combined with the gradually diminishing chain of hills on the Pamplemouse side of the town, are all well seen in the purple light of the departing sun.

I was much struck on this occasion with the beauty and truth of some remarks I had once read and noted, regarding the climate and scenery of Sicily. They were to the effect that "the charm of southern landscape depends not solely on the romantic or beautiful features which enter into its composition. In that land of the sun, the purity of the atmosphere, the rich and magical lines of colour, the softness of the aëreal perspective, the powerful relief of lights and shadows, produce impressions of pleasure, rarely equalled, even in our finest days," in northern regions.

With equal accuracy might this have been written of the charming view of "la belle Maurice" that fascinated us on the occasion referred to.

As soon as the bell buoy at the mouth of the harbour was passed, we steered along the ridge of reefs leading to the embouchure of Grand River, bringing into view the well cultivated districts of Moka and Plain Wilhelms with their romantic ravines, variegated villas, bright green patches of cane cultivation, and the weather side of the Port Louis mountains. These are flanked in the distance by the Trois Mammelles, and other hills towards the district of Savanne, ending in a bold, bluff rock, separated from the main land and forming the most southerly point of the island.

Some of our party were engaged in watching the signals of recognition hoisted at their fast-fading homes, and exchanging invisible salutations with the dear ones so recently left behind. The ladies in the Mauritius are as well versed in Marryat's code, and the distinctive flags of the island, as were the romantic heroines of Cooper's Pilot in the telegraph established with their naval sweet-hearts. Others, like myself, then birds of passage and citizens of the world without local ties, were partly occupied in enjoying the ever-varying, and always poetical tints of the pretty panorama coloured by the chameleon rays of the setting sun; and in part in scanning the movements and appearance of our fellow-travellers. The fresh breeze and short pitching sea that met us as soon as we were clear of the influence of the land, speedily prostrated the major portion of the company, few of whom again raised their heads before the completion of our pilgrimage.

The deck of the little steamer was completely choked with bags of coal, intended to aid her in towing up the wreck of the Blythswood, the object of her passage down. The cabins below were so insufferably hot and stifling, that I doubt if even that modern salamander, Chabert, the fire king, could have withstood their temperature for half an hour, without being reduced to the state of the ancient nymphs in Sicily, when by some mysterious and potent influence they dissolved into liquid fountains.

My good friends had unfortunately carried off the remainder of the fat turkey on which we had tiffed before quitting the land, and as I had been unmindful of the sage maxim of Dugald Dalgettie to 'victual myself for three days,' I ran a serious risk of dining with Duke Humphrey, or partaking of a Barmecide repast in the presence of those more prudent and provident than myself. From this dilemma I was saved by the hospitable kindness of the chief of our party—a fine specimen of the genuine old John Bull type of gentleman—an old retired naval officer, who had long since converted his log-book into a ledger. His womankind—reminding me that I was far away from mine—furnished him as plentifully with 'vivers and munition' as did the dainty dame of Gilpin for his famous ride. Of this I derived the benefit, and on the succeeding day breakfasted and tiffed in a Sybarite fashion with another good Samaritan of the same stamp, with a young wife at home.

The early part of the night was clear, and the heavens were studded with the bright stars of the southern hemisphere. I had long essayed in vain to court the drowsy god upon an uneasy couch composed of two moveable coal sacks with a small cask between them, and had scarcely dozed off, amidst all possible varieties of sounds caused by the demon of sea-sickness among those scattered around, when I was suddenly awoke by an awful bang, followed by a stentorian shout of "Hard down with your helm, you fool!"

The gentle moon had now arisen and cast her pale silver light upon the scene, fleecy masses of cloud were scudding rapidly across her disk, and the steamer was taken aback, tossed about like a cockle-shell on the troubled waters. It was difficult to imagine at first what had gone wrong, from the confusion worse confounded that immediately arose. Some thought we had struck upon a rock and were settling fast, whilst others imagined that the boiler was about to burst. Amidst cries of 'Mourir pour la patrie,' 'wallop your jackass,' and other strange ejaculations, order was restored, when it was discovered that the wheel and its guardians had got drunk on genuine liberty, equality, and fraternity principles, and mistaking the North for the South, were steering us back to our starting point.

It is but fair to the worthy little skipper of the craft, a steady, careful seaman, rejoicing in the soubriquet of 'Old swear-hard' from a vile pun on his patronymic, to mention, that the irregularities began after he left the deck at midnight, and that no one informed him of the catastrophe until it was past praying for.

Our gallant old commodore took the command, and soon set matters to rights, but it was long before sleep again visited us, broken as it was by the running fire of wit, strange sounds, and aching peals of laughter, that rung from time to time in uncontrollable bursts across the deck. Few who were there, will readily forget the exquisitely ludicrous humours of that night; to convey a picture of them to others is impossible.

At dawn of day we were astir and on the look out for Bourbon, which appeared like a huge, light blue, faintly traced mountain, towering above the horizon. At sun-rise when our distance could not have been short of forty miles or more, the sharp crest of the Salazie was distinctly visible, and the whole outline of the island easily made out.

But where was our friend the Églé? The horizon was scanned in every direction, and one among us fancied he made her out in our wake; this turned out to be a delusion, for she was speedily discovered many miles a head, racing along like a skimmer of the seas, under a small pyramid of canvass. She shortly disappeared under the shadow of the mountainous mass towards which we were steering.

Long and tedious was our approach. The 'Prince Albert,' although a neatly built boat, was but a coal tub after all, and with a fair wind, favourable current, and full steam-power, made scarcely four miserable knots an hour. She is said to have engines of eighty horse-power—I doubt if they represent a force of forty donkies, so wretched was our rate of progress. Her office is to tow vessels into Port Louis harbour, and to assist ships dismasted or in danger on the coast during the hurricane months, but she is utterly unequal to the latter duty, and was once the cause of an awful catastrophe. She went out to aid a vessel in difficulty, and succeeded in putting a pilot on board, but was unable to bring her into port: she cast off the ill-starred ship, which, with her unfortunate pilot drifted out to sea, and most probably foundered, for nothing has ever been heard of them since.

The colonists sent home for another steamer, and got out a second tub, more powerful than the first, but quite as unsuited to face heavy weather; in fact a river boat fitted out for sea work.

Were the government of the Mauritius in possession of a proper steamer, of at least 250 or 300 horse power, built for the navigation of the broad ocean in bad weather, many a valuable ship and cargo would in all human probability be saved.

Had such a vessel been at the disposal of the authorities of Port Louis, the necessity for the despatch of the Prince Albert to Bourbon, would not have existed. The ill-fated Blythswood was dismasted and narrowly escaped destruction in the March cyclone, that handled so severely two other vessels from Calcutta, the Lord Nelson and the American ship Washington. The former was dismasted, had her decks swept, and came into port all but water-logged. The latter was so severely injured as to make her repairs more costly than her value; she has, therefore, I believe, been sold and probably broken up.

The Blythswood was seen under a small fore-sail rigged on a jury-mast, hovering about the island for a couple of days. At one time she was said to have been actually off the harbour of Port Louis. One of the steamers put out to render her assistance, but was driven back by stress of weather. The ship drifted to leeward and was conjectured to have foundered, when the Églé on her return from St. Denis brought up the news of her abandonment at sea, and of the captain and crew having saved themselves by taking to their boats.

The history of her being subsequently picked up by some French fishermen, of her being found in excellent condition with the exception of the loss of her masts and rudder, and of the generous, disinterested and high-minded conduct of the French Governor in regard to her, are already well known. They are besides somewhat foreign to the purposes of my 'rough notes.'

For some hours as we approached the island, it seemed to recede from us. The rising sun raised a cloud of vapour that enveloped the tops of the higher hills, and shrouded the shore in a semi-obscure mist.

About mid-day the light house of Saint Suzanne was made out, and from this time the peculiar features of the landscape gradually came into view, until at length they formed a magnificent panorama of highly cultivated coast, dotted at intervals with quaint-looking habitations, and the tall chimnies of sugar-houses, backed by a lofty range of mountains, intersected in every direction, by ragged, rugged, dark, precipitous ravines. In the far distance to the northward, appeared a delicate tracery of masts, indicating the position of the road-stead of St. Denis.

Close to the land we came up with the Églé which, after fairly beating us by more than six hours in a run of less than a hundred miles, lost her fair wind and was unable to make her anchorage. We towed her in, and came to anchor ourselves between 4 and 5 P. M. having been very nearly twenty-four hours at sea.

SAINT DENIS.

Re-union, or Bourbon, or Mascarenhas, for it delights in all these appellations, according to Horsburgh, is an island of "round form about fourteen leagues from N. W. to S. E. which is its greatest length. There is a volcano near the S. E. part, and the high-peaked mountain near the centre of the island is in about Lat. 21° 9′ S. Although this island is larger than Mauritius, it is only a great mountain, in a manner cloven through the whole height in three different places; the summit is covered with wood, and its declivity which extends to the sea, is cleared and cultivated in two-thirds of its circuit; the remainder is covered with lava of the volcano, which generally burns gently and without noise; but it is sometimes violent in the rainy season. In November, 1828, it was in a state of activity, and the summit of the mountain was visible above the horizon at ninety-seven miles distance."

Such is the brief description of it given by the celebrated hydrographer of the eastern seas.

It is, in fact, of an irregular oval form, Point des Galets in the N. W., and Point de la Table in the S. E. being the extreme limits of its greatest diameter.

It rises rapidly from its iron-bound, inhospitable coast, to its highest point, the Piton des Neiges, nearly in the centre of the isle. This snowy peak is the crest of a bold, bare, rocky ridge dividing the Cilaos from the Salazie range of mountains. It is, I believe, higher than even the summit of the volcano, and has frequently been seen on a clear day from the neighbouring island of Mauritius, at a distance very little, if anything, short of a hundred miles.

According to Bory de St. Vincent, Bourbon is composed of two volcanic mountains, originating at different and distant periods. "In the southern part, which is the smallest, the subterranean fires still commit ravages ; that of the north is much larger; the volcanic eruptions that formerly made great devastations, are now no longer in action ; species of basins, or little valleys, rapid rivers, hemmed in by perpendicular ramparts, little mountains thrown into these valleys by which their course is impeded ; basaltic prisms, often disposed as in the island of Staffa, in regular columns ; beds of lava in great variety, deep fissures that indicate a general convulsion, all attest ancient and dreadful physical revolutions. The narrow flat shore interrupted in several places is composed only, as at Teneriffe, of basaltic pebbles, or other burning lavas ; these stones are washed into the sea by the rains ; true sands are no where to be found; what is improperly called by that name is composed of calcareous rubbish and of marine bodies, thrown upon the shore by the waves, where may be seen in miniature a collection of all the lavas of the island, which the motion of the tides has reduced to very small pieces, of a bluish slaty appearance."

St. Denis, the chief town of the Island and the seat of its government, is in Lat. 20° 52′ S. Long. 55° 57′ E. It is situated at the most northerly point of the land, faces an open, exposed, shingle beach, and is built under the lee of a lofty, picturesque range of hills.

It is scarcely visible from the sea until near the anchorage ground, and then appears a small town, from most of the houses being surrounded by trees, shutting them out from a distant view.

The most remarkable objects that first strike the beholder on approaching, are, the handsome range of stone barracks, and the military hospital ; the Government House, Artillery Barrack, and public offices visible from the offing, presenting nothing very grand or picturesque.

Shortly after we had come to an anchor, a white boat, manned by half a dozen creole rowers, and containing an imposing looking personage in the stern sheets, pulled off from the landing pier. This contained the Port Surgeon, a man of no little consequence where the ancient and absurd quarantine laws are so rigidly enforced, as they are at Bourbon and in the Mauritius. He hailed us at a respectful distance, and enquired if we arrived with the very essential document known as a "Patente de Santé," or in our vulgar tongue a "bill of health." Old *Swear-hard* was called to the fore, when it turned out that he had either forgotten or neglected this necessary passport, urging that he had been down once before without one, and that as nothing had then been said about it, he deemed it of equally little use now.

This Sancho Panza sort of reasoning produced no effect upon the dogmatic disciple of Esculapius, who was equally in vain assailed with every species of argument, entreaty, and expostulation. He talked learnedly about epidemic influences, contagious catastrophes, sacred duty of preserving the public health and regulating the laws of mortality, and pulled off in high dudgeon at some of the remarks made, leaving for our consolation a parting benediction of 'five days quarantine!'

Here was a pleasant dilemma—the boat rolling incessantly in a heavy swell, coated with coal-dust from stem to stern, and no provisions on board! Then arose vain lamentations over the lost turkey, and useless sighs at the reckless, wasteful expenditure of Strasburgh pies and cold chicken.

Among the various suggestions of the moment were,—to land, storm the town, and hang the doughty doctor to the nearest lantern; to raise a simultaneous shout of 'Vive la republique,' and board the barrachois in the smoke; to up anchor and steer back for Port Louis; to make a Doctor, who happened to be on board, inspect and grant certificates of soundness to the crew and passengers; or to change the name of the island from Reunion to Separation!

The existence of these quarantine laws is, in truth, an unmitigated nuisance, and a relic of days of ignorance and idle dread, by no means creditable to the good sense or progress in knowledge of either island.

It would be useless to discuss so vexed a question here. Their acknowledged inefficacy and foundation on erroneous principles, are so fully recognized by those whose opinions should guide the public sense in such matters, as to lead to the hope that they will ere long be ranked with the Picts' wall or the Mahratta ditch, as means of keeping out an enterprizing and formidable enemy.

In the midst of our tribulation, a magical little piece of bunting was hoisted at the flag staff, and received with a cheer of delight. It was an intimation that the coast was clear, and that we were at liberty to land as soon as we liked. For this we had to thank the sensible and kind-hearted Governor.

At the time of our arrival there were some eight or ten ships in the roadstead, among them an armed transport, and the floating hull of the Blythswood.

The place of disembarkation was an iron pier or barrachois, projected beyond the line of breakers on the beach, and continuous with the Rue de Paris, the principal street of the town. A ladder was let down alongside of the pier, exactly like that of a large ship, and the passengers and luggage passed up it, very much as they enter the Haddington steamer in the Madras roads. The charge for each person, including baggage, was ten francs, the regulated police tariff of the place.

While we were taking up our position, and during our landing, a large crowd of spectators lined the shore. Immediately on placing foot on the planking of the pier, evidences of being in a foreign land presented themselves, and I was strongly reminded of my first visit to France some twenty-one years ago. There were the same green coated, bearded, armed Custom House officers, looking as if time had stood still, and no change had passed over the fair face of *la belle France*. There were the stalwart Gens D'Armes, and the blue-coated foot soldiers, with their long, bright-barrelled muskets, and slouching, careless gait, very much as they used to be in the good old days of the citizen king.

We were marched off under the charge of a couple of searchers, through whose hands our baggage was speedily passed, and by whom we were treated with much civility and politeness.

The custom houses of Bourbon and Mauritius are well-ordered institutions, in which every stranger is regarded as an honest man and a gentleman, instead of being roughly handled as if he were a smuggler or a thief —the practice of some other places through which it was erst my lot to pass.

There are two Hotels in St. Denis, that of Joinville, on the Place du Gouvernement, the one to which we went, and which is chiefly frequented by the commanders of ships and bachelors : the other, the Hotel d'Europe, situated in the town and resorted to by families, as well as the better class of the inhabitants. The latter is undoubtedly the best arranged, and has the best cuisine ; the objections to it are, its position and the existence of a café which is usually open to a late hour. Both are comparatively moderate in their charges, and superior to the establishments at Port Louis, one of which at least, is expensive and ill-conducted, the master being inattentive and above his business, the servants lazy and impudent, and the table indifferent. Visitors from India should bear this in mind, and especially not neglect to make a *pucka* agreement with the maitre d'hotel before taking up their quarters, or they will be treated as I was.

After endeavouring in a warm bath to scrub off the coal dust of the Steamer, we sat down to dinner at the table d'hôte, at which the greatest novelty to me was a dish of wild strawberries and cream. Subsequently to this our English party had a separate table, in which we were not particularly well treated. Fish and poultry are usually good in Bourbon, butcher's meat dear and indifferent. The market is fairly supplied with such fruits and vegetables as are in season. Among the former, during our stay, were custard apples, plantains, bananas, oranges in great variety, pine-apples, alligator or avocado pears, strawberries, and occasionally grapes, the two latter rather poor and tasteless. The mangoes, mangosteens, guavas, and leechees of the island are said to be particularly fine. All the fruits are better flavoured than those of Bengal.

St. Denis being situated on the declivity of the surrounding hills, gradually rises from the sea beach to the upper part of the town, which is bounded by the bases of the mountain range in that direction. Such is also, but in a minor degree, the nature of the site of Port Louis, and to this circumstance is doubtless due much of the cleanliness and excellent drainage of the two towns.

The streets of St. Denis are placed diagonally nearly north and south, and are intersected at almost equal distances by cross streets running east and west.

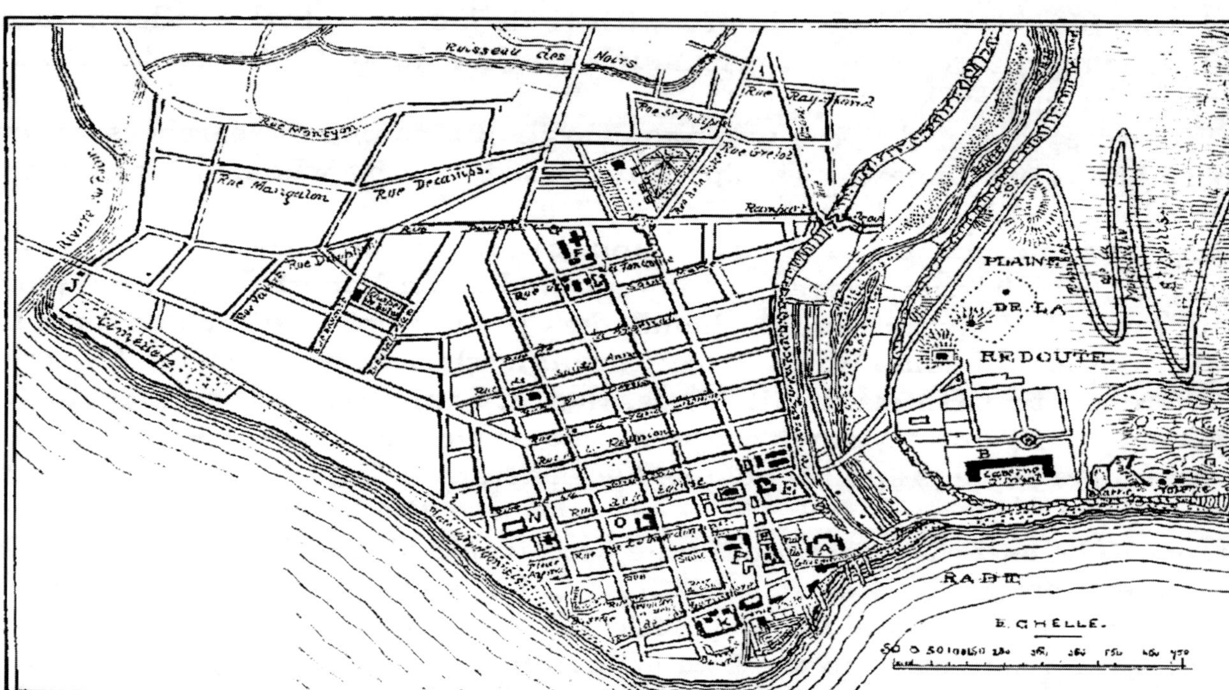

Upon its eastern aspect the town is built on the side of the ravine leading to the canal des moulins and river of St. Denis, the latter a shallow, rocky-bedded stream, emptying itself into the sea near the centre of the anchorage ground. The road here is cut in zig-zag parallels ending in a solid substantial bridge leading to the plaine de la Redoute, race course, infantry barrack, and mountain of St. Denis, on which stands the signal station. On its eastern aspect the town is bounded by the Riviére du Butor. Near its embouchure is the great cemetery, running along the sea shore—a fit spot for the receptacle of the dead, lulled by the ceaseless roar of the mighty ocean near its foot. There is something very solemn and suggestive of meditation, in the enclosure, its peculiarly French mode of decoration and distribution, and its singularly well chosen site. What better emblem of eternity can be imagined than the sleepless, perpetual motion of the ever-rolling wave as it breaks upon the pebbly beach, whether in the gentle ripple of a calm starlight night, or the sullen stunning roar of the awful surf, during the angry strife of the elements in the devastating hurricane.

The most interesting tomb to an Englishman, however, is one erected on the plaine de la Redoute, in the form of an obelisk to the memory of an officer, named Frazer, who was killed in the capture of the island, and with some hundred others, is said to be buried beneath the monument. A more romantic and appropriate spot for a soldier's grave could scarcely have been selected. I accidentally, during my stay in Reunion, fell in with a pleasant, kind-hearted old gentleman, who was in the island at the time of its capture, and knew the man by whom Frazer was shot.

The gallant Scot was a mounted officer, and conspicuous from the distinguished manner in which he was leading on his men—the tirailleur marked and killed him from the neighbouring heights. Many traits of gallantry and good feeling on both sides are preserved by the older members of the community, who still remember the luxury, fine horses, and brilliant equipments of the invading force.

One anecdote of those by-gone days which I heard from a lady who was present on the occasion to which she referred, exhibited in no very favorable light the civilization of old Anglo-Indians of the Nabob school, so graphically immortalized by the most poetical and dramatic of historians.

Colonel Keating, the British Governor of Bourbon after its conquest, was an eccentric, but, in his way, hospitable man. At one of his great state dinners the ladies had retired to the drawing-room, leaving their lords to the enjoyment of the bottle and the hookah, post-prandial performances, now happily more honoured in the breach than the observance.

The denizens of St. Denis have always been celebrated for their skill as musicians, and their taste for harmony and melody. The lady of the island chief proposed to her gentle guests to pass the weary interval in the exercise of this most humanizing of social arts. The piano was opened, the most brilliant of its chords struck, and the liquid notes of the local Jenny Lind poured forth, when a pencil missive from the Tartar in the lower regions arrested the concord of sweet sounds. It was couched in the coarsest terms, bidding the ladies, literally in the terms of Tom Thumb's address to his brave army, "not to kick up a row!"

The impression produced by this Oriento-gothic barbarism has scarcely been softened down by an interval of thirty years.

The houses in St. Denis are generally built of wood, with sloping, barn-like, shingle roofs, and occasionally a basement of basalt. They are enclosed in small gardens laid out with much taste and effect. The interiors are usually simple and neat, with polished floors, papered walls, and European furniture and ornaments. Some few are decorated with considerable taste, and successful pretensions to architectural elegance, especially that of a Monsieur

Manès in the Rue de Paris; the majority, however, to a visitor from India, appear small, confined, and ill-ventilated. All are more or less disfigured by the heavy storm shutters used both here and in the Mauritius as a protection against hurricanes.

The real comforts of an English residence are entirely wanting, and I doubt if there is such a thing as a good bathing room in the whole of Bourbon. They are almost equally scarce at the Mauritius, the only really good baths that I saw being the glorious one at Reduit, a Naiad's fountain at Plains Wilhelms, and the river at Burnside. At the hotels baths form an extra item of expenditure, and although good of their kind, do not by any means realize our Indian notions of cleanliness and propriety in this all-essential regard.

In Bourbon, as also in the sister isle, in the public rooms of the hotels, and the chief apartments of many of the houses, the walls are covered with coloured paper, representing all possible varieties of landscapes, costumes, scenery, battle pieces, and similar devices. The majority of them are very coarsely executed, but produce a pleasing effect at a little distance. The best that fell under my observation were well known and familiar scenes from the life of Napoleon, whose memory seems to be regarded with much respect and attachment even in this distant corner of the world.

Some of the public buildings are excellent, and constructed on a scale of liberality; others are small, but probably well adapted for their special purposes. The Government House is a neat and commodious dwelling-

house, facing the sea, with a miniature garden and terrace in front. It has a dwarf cupola in its centre, neither ornamental nor imposing, and the state rooms, although elegant and well-furnished, are scarcely large enough for the reception of so numerous a community. All connected with it is, however, in extremely good taste, and such as to impress a stranger with the most favorable estimate of its hospitable and excellent inmates. Although architecturally more elegant, it is neither so commodious, nor so handsomely fitted up, as the barn-like casket which enshrines the representative of royalty in Port Louis. The national flag is hoisted on the cupola on Sundays, holidays, and all great state occasions.

The great glory of the town is the handsome Infantry barrack, which is scarcely finished, as it has at present no officers' quarters attached to it.

It is executed with a degree of consideration for the health, comfort and efficiency of the soldiers lodged in it, that reflects much credit on the wisdom and liberality of the French Government. It is scarcely possible to imagine how any other feeling should ever regulate arrangements for the well-being of such valuable and expensive agents as European troops, in distant, and more especially tropical colonies. The site being well chosen, the difference of a few additional cubic feet of fresh air for each man, with the comparatively small proportional outlay in buildings, makes all the distinction between a healthy and an unhealthy barrack. The ultimate cost of an error in the economical direction is not to be calculated in money alone,—although the loss even in this sordid sense is enormous—but in the awful destruction of human life that has been so frequently and fatally witnessed in the east. The trained and acclimated soldier is not readily replaced by the raw recruit, nor can his needless sacrifice be justified by any argument of economy.

The Infantry Barrack of St. Denis is a long range of stone building, two-storied, and not unlike that of Chinsurah, except that it has small wings projecting from its extremities on the sea face. It has broad verandahs running the whole length of the structure, on the same side, large enough to muster the guards, and to serve for all interior parades and inspections in wet weather.

The rooms are large, well-ventilated, and admirably arranged, each soldier having an abundance of space. His kit is upon a small shelf above his head, and the arm racks are neatly arranged around central pillars. This is a superior means of disposing of them to the disfigurement of the walls along which they are usually placed in Indian barracks. The stands are arranged high above the ground, and each niche is marked with the name and number of the soldier to whom the musket belongs. There are twenty-six beds in each room, and the dining tables of the men run between them in the centre of the apartment. Above the tables are suspended from the ceiling, safes for provisions, and gogglets of drinking water. The cleanliness, cheerful and airy appearance of the whole, are all that could be desired.

The Serjeant Major and Colour Serjeant of each company have separate rooms, on the doors of which their names and numbers are inscribed.

The building contains, in addition, the offices of the staff of the corps, a magazine for clothing and accoutrements, and another for arms and ammunitions, both complete and as perfect as such departments can be made. There are, also, on the ground floor a range of solitary cells, and above, the regimental school-room. This with a salle d'escrime or fencing room to the right of the great entrance, completes the details of the main building.

Immediately opposite the main entrance of the barrack, and detached from it, is the regimental kitchen, constructed upon a simple and efficient plan, worthy of universal adoption. It is either a circular or polygonal building, I forget exactly which, and around a central chimney are arranged the cooking apparatus of every company in the regiment, each distinct from the other, and presided over by its special functionary. The cook is a soldier of the company and exempt from all ordinary regimental duties. The culinary machinery consists of a large iron pan, in which meat is stewed under a slight degree of pressure, on the principle of a chemical digester, and of two or three saucepans. The stoves are on the same principle as the chulahs of a well furnished Anglo-Indian kitchen. The soup preparing for the men at the time of our visit was excellent, and as unlike as possible to the black broth of the republican soldiers of ancient Greece; seldom have I tasted it so well made in India, even in the houses of the great.

The most interesting probably of all the departments, are the school and fencing rooms. Both are under the charge of the same officer, Lieutenant Vallière, the kind and accomplished individual who accompanied us in our visit. The extent of instruction to which the non-commissioned officers are carried in mathematical and general attainments, is considerably beyond the standard recently adopted by the Horse Guards for the admission and promotion of officers in the Queen's army. Attendance in the school is compulsory both to privates and non-commissioned officers, so that there is not a single individual in the corps unable to read and write, while many in the ranks are well read and highly informed individuals. One of these I subsequently fell in with on sick leave at a distance from his regiment, and it was delightful to witness the extent and accuracy of his information on all subjects which form the ordinary staple of conversation in educated society.

It is this refinement and intellectuality which stamps its peculiar features on the French soldiery, and renders them such ready and effective troops. The soldier and non-commissioned officer know as much as those who are leading them; the object and nature of every movement and manœuvre are thoroughly understood by them. Thence in the manner of execution, much is left to the discretion and sense of the soldier. The result is less mechanical perfection than obtains in armies where the men are mere animated machines, and entirely dependent on the superior knowledge of their officers. But, in spite of what appears to us the careless and ill-disciplined manner, in which the French soldier marches and manœuvres, there is much to admire in him. He is perfectly acquainted with his duty, can take advantage of every cover and eminence afforded by the ground on which he is acting, and if need be, march and wheel as steadily as even the Russian regiments which struck the Duke of Wellington so much in the celebrated review of the Emperor Alexander, in 1816.

The fencing school is an institution unknown to our infantry branch of the service. The room in which it is held at St. Denis is adorned with the cartoons of some regimental Raphael, chiefly representing armorial devices, and the idolatry of the French army for their great Emperor. Every soldier is obliged to pass through this school, in which the broad-sword and single stick are interdicted, as tending to spoil the hand and wrist, for the cunning fence of carte and tierce.

Lieut. Vallière also presides over the target practice, but this we had not an opportunity of witnessing.

Notwithstanding the general air of carelessness and indifference with which the French soldier appears to perform his duties, and the amount of licence to manage matters in his own way which is undoubtedly left to him, the reins of discipline are as firmly held and as tightly drawn as in our own army. There is no leaven of liberty and equality allowed to intrude here. The sentry may hold his firelock as he chooses, the guard may amuse themselves at cards or dominoes, and the details of the drill may be accompanied by the running commentaries of the recruit, yet are all the essential duties of the soldier exacted with a rigour that admits of no relaxation.

In looking out of our verandah one morning during a heavy shower of rain, we witnessed an amusing method of relieving the sentry at the gate of the governor's house. The '*factionnaire*' was snugly ensconced in his box to which the next for duty ran as fast as his legs could carry him, leaving his firelock in the guard-room ; the relieved sentinel returned in the same summary manner, transferring his musket to his successor, and the whole appeared to be taken as a matter of course, the non-commissioned officers sanctioning the proceeding, or at least not interfering to prevent it.

The true secret of the facility with which discipline is maintained, even in a republican force, is in the large amount of individual power and responsibility invested in the officers. This increases with the rank of the individual, and may be exercised at once. The confirmation, mitigation, or increase of any punishment which he may order, rests with the commanding officer of the regiment, over whom a power of supervision is again exercised by the military commandant of the island. The authority of the Captain of a company in some respects is as great as that of a commanding officer in the British army, and the power of the Lieutenant-Colonel in some particulars, with us could only be exercised by a Court Martial. The centralization system which converts a Commander-in-chief into a 'monster adjutant,' and renders the officers of a regiment nearly powerless, is unknown, and wisely so too, considering the materials of which the French army is composed. The policy of such a system with any troops is questionable, and has been supposed by officers of experience to have been the cause of some modern mutinies and military executions.

The danger of entrusting extensive power to individuals is doubtless great, if they should happen not to be men of temper, discretion, and judgment. The French officers as a body are so well acquainted with their duties, that instances of exceeding their authority or of awarding unsuitable and improper punishment are said to be extremely rare ; and if they do happen, are only in trivial, unimportant matters.

The uniform of the marine battalion at present quartered in Reunion is more suitable for a tropical climate than our own. It consists of a double-breasted blue frock-coat, full in the skirts, and worn open on the upper part of the chest, with full, loose white trowsers, gaiters, and for the men worsted epaulettes. The cap is almost as elegant and not very unlike our present infantry tschako, with a worsted tuft; it is lighter than the English cap, and capable of resisting a sabre cut.

The men are all armed with bright-barrelled percussion muskets, and the old Roman sword. The cross-belt has been abolished in the French army, and is supplied by a couple of straps, which are rapidly adjusted, leave the arms perfectly free, and exercise no injurious pressure on the chest.

There is another and older barrack for the infantry in the town on the Place de l'Eglise, near the military hospital. In it the flank companies are lodged. Besides these, there are special barracks for the gens d'Armes and artillery. The former is an imposing but ricketty-looking old wooden building; the latter I did not visit.

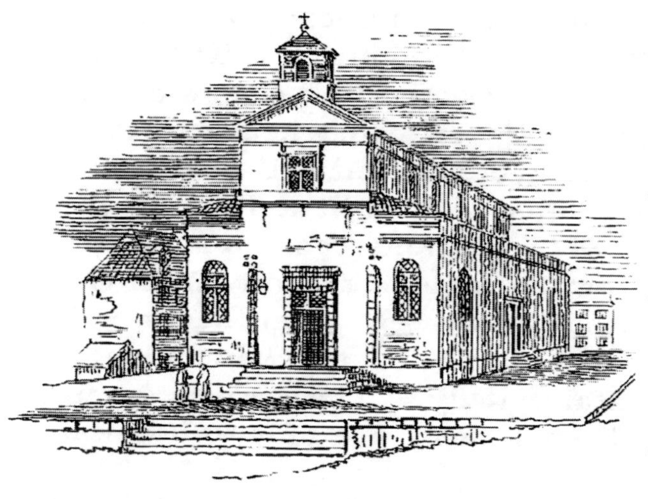

There are three Churches in St. Denis, the principal one in the Place de l'Eglize, and the others, the chapel of the Assumption attached to and adjoining the College, and the Butor chapel. None of them possess any claim to architectural elegance or beauty of any sort. In the former are a few very indifferent paintings and ugly prints, unworthy of description or special notice. A Roman Catholic Bishop has recently been appointed to preside over the ecclesiastical establishments of the island. He had not arrived from France at the time of our visit.

The slaughter-house of St. Denis is built on the distant bank of the river and the sea shore: it is a plain, substantial building, well-adapted for its purpose, and removed far enough from human habitations to prevent the offals of the slaughtered animals causing any injurious effect upon the public health.

Why Calcutta, which so much more needs it, is without such an essential structure, it is not for me to say. Medical Police is little known and valued among us at home or abroad.

The hospitals of the town abut on the edge of the ravine leading down to the river, and are situated in the Rue de Paris, near the church. The chief of them is a large three-storied building, recently erected, the centre of the military hospital of which the wings are in course of construction. It is planned on the same scale as the barrack and when completed will be a noble institution. The wards are long, large, and lofty, but a little too narrow. Each patient has a considerable allowance of room, and the whole is well ventilated. At the time of my visit it was crowded with sick, many from the garrison, but the greater number of the serious cases were from the French settlements in Madagascar. These were chiefly victims of the worst type of pernicious remittent fever, a fearful and fatal malady. There was a spacious ward for officers, all of whom in the French army are sent to hospital for treatment when sick.

The service of the hospital is performed by a large staff of medical officers, ruled over by a chief with rank and duties corresponding to those of our superintending surgeon.

The Palais de Justice or Supreme Court of the Island, is situated in a large-walled enclosure near the upper end of the town between the Rue de la Fontaine and the Rue Ste. Márie. It is a substantial, three-storied building, formerly a dwelling house, and contains the several courts recognized in French jurisprudence. The barristers practise in all the courts, and the judges are very numerous, being no less than thirteen in number in the court of appeal alone. Its proceedings are conducted exactly as in similar courts in France, the judgment of the court being usually given in writing.

The love of litigation appears to be as radically ingrained in the Creole population of Bourbon, as it is in the Normans and Bretons of the old country, or in the natives of India. The law is consequently a flourishing profession

at St. Denis, and among its members, are, as usual, some of the most enlightened, amiable, and excellent members of the community.

The education of the male part of the better classes of the population is entirely in the hands of the government, and is at present, so far as I can learn, confined to a large central college, or '*Lycée Colonial*' in St. Denis.

This is a school of secondary instruction, conducted on exactly the same footing in regard to study, discipline, and organization, as the colleges in France that form part of the university. It is under the control of the Director of the Interior, in subordination to the Commissary General of the Republic.

The college is a large building, situated near to the public garden at the upper end of the town. It has several court-yards or distinct play-grounds for different classes of pupils, and is enclosed by high walls.

The building is commodious and capable of affording instruction to four or five hundred pupils. There is scarcely more than half that number in the institution at present, the recent emancipation of the slaves without any immediate remuneration, having ruined a large number of landholders and of the more respectable classes, of whom they formed the chief wealth.

The immediate control of this national institution is vested in a resident *Proviseur* or Principal, assisted by a censor, a domestic chaplain, an econome or purveyor, with professors and maitres d'etudes, or directors of the private studies of the pupils, a class of functionaries unknown to our secular schools.

The principal, censor, and professors are nominated and appointed by the minister of Marine and the Colonies, the remaining functionaries are appointed by the colonial authorities in whom this patronage is vested.

The proviseur is the head of the institution, which he controls and manages in all departments subject to certain regulations for his guidance. He also acts in all unforeseen and urgent cases, reporting his proceedings to the director of the interior.

The censor is the special and immediate authority in all matters relating to study and discipline. He acts for the principal during his absence from whatever cause.

The chaplain is charged with the religious duties of the Lyceum, the purveyor with all relating to its provision and furniture, and the chief medical officer of the island attends the sick, for whom there is a comfortable infirmary in the building.

The professors and all employed are liable to dismissal or suspension from rank, pay, and allowances for "faits portant scandal ou blessant la delicatesse ou l'honnêteté," according to the gravity of the offence. They are likewise precluded from entering into any other occupation, except that of teaching out-door pupils under the sanction of the principal.

The regulations regarding prizes, holidays, and similar matters are the same in principle as those of our education department, differing only in some unimportant details.

The course of education embraces the study of Greek and Latin, French and English, Philosophy, History, the Mathematical and Physical Sciences and Drawing. Dancing, Fencing, and Music may also be learned, but form no necessary part of the college course. Candidates are prepared for the Polytechnic School in Paris.

I went through the various classes and departments of the institution with the proviseur, a young man of energy, learning, and much kindliness and courtesy of manner, who evidently is much loved and respected by all under his charge. The college appeared to me to be admirably conducted, and in first rate order.

When at Port Louis I had an opportunity of visiting the Royal College of Mauritius, but unfortunately did not see the classes at work. It appears to be a well-organized, flourishing institution, and must doubtless be a great boon to the better classes of the colonial population, who are unable or unwilling to send their children to Europe for education.

The great mistake that seems to me to have been committed in the Mauritius both in its system of education and in the government of the colony, is the undue prominence given to the French language. As soon as it became an English possession, the English language should at once have been made the medium of all official communications and ordinances, should have been introduced into the courts of law, and should have been notified as the future language of the country. That it would have been attended with much inconvenience and very many difficulties in the first instance is undoubted; but time, patience, and judicious firmness in the ruling powers, would have overcome these, probably even before the existing generation had passed away, and the unfriendly feelings always existing in a conquered country had been forgotten, in the mildness, equity, and fostering influence of a paternal and peaceful rule.

It will be a harder task to revolutionize the island in this respect now, than it would have been in 1810. Then, all existing rights being respected and maintained in accordance with the law under which they were acquired, would have satisfied the people of the uprightness and good intentions of their conquerors, while they could not reasonably have objected to the *future* being regulated by the laws, customs, and language of the new ruling power.

The adoption of the contrary system has kept alive an irritable, vicious, unsettled foreign feeling, that will never be extinguished so long as the sympathies of the major part of the population are French. This has been the cause of most of the difficulties that have disturbed Lower Canada for so many years, and still render in so hard to manage. There exist in such a state opposing interests and conflicting feelings, which it is impossible to hope to reconcile. The Gordian knot should be cut, to untie or unravel it is impossible.

Every fresh importation from France adds fuel to the flame, and there can be little doubt that in the event of a war with that country, the government would have a domestic, as well as a foreign enemy to watch, and perhaps, to subdue.

Rigorous measures are always unpalatable and will be resisted if any hope of success is felt, but it is always wise in the long run to exercise the full right of conquest, remembering only that the sword of the conqueror should be tempered with justice and mercy.

The Romans of old and the Americans of modern times managed these matters better than we do, and in consequence felt and feel comparatively little of the annoyances which have embarrassed us, even in India. In California the Spanish tongue was immediately superseded by the Saxon dialect.

The BOTANIC GARDEN or Jardin de la Republique, still, in general, inadvertently mentioned by most people as the 'King's Garden,' is situated at the upper end of the town, but does not cover a very large area of ground.

It is under the charge of one of the most amiable, gifted, and single-minded philosophers whom it has been my good fortune to fall in with, a Monsieur Richard. His name is not unknown to fame as a scientific botanist, but the patriarchal simplicity of his habits, his unbounded kindness and anxiety to be useful, and the vast stores of information of which he seems to be an almost unconscious possessor, require to be personally witnessed to cause a thorough appreciation of his excellence. Vegetating upon a miserable stipend, and with an establishment of idle, ignorant labourers scarcely numerically equal to the mere weeding and watering of a portion of the grounds, it is still a delightful spot to visit and full of interest to every lover of the most poetical and charming department of natural history.

Monsieur Richard has arranged a section of his garden according to the natural system, where many rare and curious plants, particularly from Madagascar, may be seen. It is very rich in palms, and contains every known variety of the sugar cane.

It presents a striking contrast, restricted as are M. Richard's means of maintaining it on an efficient footing, with the pretty and poetical wilderness called the Botanical Garden, at Pamplemouse in the Mauritius. The vicinity of the tomb of Paul and Virginia, and the garden itself with its formal walks and straight avenues, dilapidated statue of Flora, and quaint old cumbrous seats, will always be interesting spots to the stranger; but the existing state of what might with comparatively little outlay be rendered a small paradise, is much to be regretted. The present gardener, honest and obliging Mr. Duncan, has done his best, and with some success, but he is not a scientific botanist, many highly interesting plants are not identified, and the means at his disposal are not such as to enable him to put it in thorough order.

Even as a means of distributing economic or ornamental plants throughout the island, of conducting interesting experiments in horticulture or agriculture, and of furnishing the means of studying Botany to such of the rising generation in the colony as are given to so elegant and useful a pursuit, it is worthy of being maintained on a better and more creditable footing out of the surplus revenue of this flourishing and prosperous island.

The vanille and chocolate plants flourish in both islands—coffee and cinnamon grow well in them, and almost every variety of tropical fruit is found in perfection. The mangosteen, mango, and pine-apple in particular, are said to be very fine; they were not in season at the time of my visit.

Formerly cotton, corn, cloves, nutmegs, canella and coffee were cultivated in Reunion.* The first was abandoned in consequence of the destruction of the plant by an incurable disease, of which the true nature was not made out. The sugar cultivation which has now nearly, if not quite, driven all other economic plants out of the field, was also threatened with extinction a few years since by a blight in the white cane. The substitution of the red cane throughout the plantations seems to have banished the epidemic for the present, and the island is just beginning to revive from the depressing effect of the visitation.

Maize and potatoes are still extensively cultivated.

By far the best kept garden in the Mauritius that I saw is at Reduit, the Governor's seat in the Moka district, which, with its fine lawn, shaded walks, romantic ravines and waterfall, well-cultivated flower beds, pretty fountain,

---

* Malte-Brun's Geography.

and level race-course, form as interesting an abode for the representative of the Sovereign, as prince or potentate could desire. The fine view of the neighbouring hills and country, with its cool and elevated site, are not the least of its recommendations, nor will those who have ridden on his back readily forget the huge, venerable, ante-diluvian old tortoise, who wanders about the grounds, a type of sober steadiness and deliberation, sadly opposed to the mercurial vivacity of this age of electricity, steam, and progress.

There is a neat little theatre at St. Denis, which is closed at present, but a well selected company is shortly expected to enliven the town. The race course is on the plaine de la Redoute, and the running is said sometimes to have been spirited and good; but both here and in the Mauritius, this interesting and useful recreation would seem to have declined of late years. The races are usually held, I believe, in October towards the end of the cold weather. The course is in a most picturesque spot, and completely commanded by the heights around, which impart an air of grandeur to the scenery, singularly pleasing to the eye of one so long confined to the dead level of the alluvial plains of Bengal, as I had been.

The regimental band plays every Sunday and Thursday evening from 8 to 10 on the place du Gouvernement, when it becomes a favorite place of resort. The scene is singular and a mimic representation of what I had frequently witnessed in France some years since. The band was almost exclusively composed of brass wind instruments, and guarded by armed sentries and gens d'armes—the spectators promenading round outside, or seated in benches under the trees bordering the upper end of the place. Around were little stalls for the sale of sweetmeats, fruits, and the small tipple usually indulged in on such occasions. A large number of soldiers off duty were scattered about the ground, and playing all sorts of practical jokes on each other, like a parcel of wild overgrown school-boys. The nights were so dark during our stay as to render it extremely difficult to distinguish individuals, but this lent its peculiar character to the scene, and gave it an air of singularity and romance that a brighter light might possibly have dispelled.

The Creoles of both islands are passionately fond of dancing, and masked and other balls are frequent during the carnival season. There was one public ball during our visit, that of the fête of the Revolution, given by the Governor on the 6th of May in the Government House. It corresponds to our Queen's birth-day ball in Calcutta. It was an elegant and animated party, exhibited a tolerably favorable display of youth and beauty, and was kept up with much spirit from eight o'clock in the evening until four, the next morning.

The ladies were arranged in double tiers around the dancing-rooms, the mammas, aunts and chaperons being in the second row, the gay animated dancers in the first rank. Polkas, waltzes, and quadrilles succeeded each other in regular succession, but the rooms were too crowded for any great display of Terpsichorean excellence. Among the best dancers of the party was an ingenuous youth of our party, termed by some of the ladies in the room—the best judges of such matters—'le jolie garçon de Maurice.' The waltz and polka appeared to me to be much less animated and rapid than those of our Indian ball-rooms; the little space for quick movement was probably the cause.

There was no formal supper—light refreshments were perpetually handed about during the evening, among them small glasses of beer, and soup in tea cups. Nothing could possibly exceed the kindness and attention to every one of the host and hostess, nor could any such party be more successful in its issue.

There is a dancing party every fortnight, less numerous and more select, upon the plan of the 'At Homes' of Miss Eden, which have been so much missed by the young people of Calcutta since Lord Auckland left India.

As in France, no introductions are necessary in the ball-room, and the ladies are handed back to their seats directly each dance is completed; in the latter respect, I imagine, that our English fashion is more approved by the fair portion of the creation.

It was our good fortune two days after our arrival at St. Denis, to witness a grand review of all the regular troops in garrison, amounting to about a thousand men. The display took place on the Plaine de la Redoute, a large level space at the foot of a range of very lofty hills, intersected by deep picturesque ravines.

The infantry were divided into two battalions, with a small battery of foot artillery, and a few fine tall gens d'armes to represent the mounted arm of the mimic army. We drove to the ground in a hired carriage a little before four in the afternoon, and found the roads crowded with gaily dressed pedestrians, all wending their way in the same direction. The plain was dotted with groups of spectators, and the troops had already taken up their position, infantry on the right flank, artillery in the centre, the cavalry on the left flank. Upon the top of a little eminence commanding the field was a handsome pavilion, in which the fair members of the gentle sex were assembled to view the parade. To this we had received a kind invitation from Colonel de Barolet, the military commandant of the Island, a tall, handsome soldierly man, in the prime of life, full of energy and activity, and a very strict disciplinarian. A small, separate pavilion was assigned to the ladies of the Governor and their party, which struck us as rather an anti-republican distinction of ranks, which are supposed to have merged into the general body of democracy.

An officer, Lt. Vallière, was on duty to conduct the ladies to their seats, and the ground around the tents was kept by a couple of sentinels.

Shortly after our arrival a company of sailors from the war steamer Archimedes, marched to the ground preceded by the rattle of the brass drum:

they were marched up the heights to take possession of a small battery on the summit of the signal mountain.

Precisely at four o'clock, the firing of a gun announced the approach of the Governor, who drove up in a carriage, and was received on alighting by the staff on foot, the only mounted individual present, with the exception of the dragoons, some 30 or 40 in number, being the Lieutenant-Colonel commanding the parade.

The usual rattle of drums, braying of trumpets, and presentation of arms took place when His Excellency with the staff walked down the line and inspected the men. They then took up a central position and the manœuvring began. The marching, counter-marching, throwing out of skirmishers, charge of cavalry, support of infantry, formation of squares, advance and retreat, and similar movements were well and duly performed, interspersed and enlivened with the firing of great and small guns. The coup-d'œil and effect at this time were very fine. Wreaths of white smoke floated in the pure air of a cloudless sky, magnificent shadows and tints were thrown from the surrounding hills by the setting sun, and a deep rolling, repeated echo, increased an hundred-fold the solemn thunder of the cannon, and the sharp rattle of the musketry. To my perception the best executed movements of the day were, the advance of the skirmishers, and the formation of echelon squares with guns at the angles. The marching and firing were both excellent, and proved the troops to be in a high state of efficiency. A singular and pretty diversion was caused by the firing of the sailors from the elevated battery, a flash with small curling wreaths of smoke being visible some time before the faint sound of the distant report reached the ear.

After more than an hour's duration of this mimic war the troops piled arms and scattered themselves about the ground, the Governor and his staff with the officers present, came to the pavilion, and the band was brought up to enliven us with its martial strains. Cakes and wine were handed round to the ladies, and an abundance of champagne and excellent cheer was meted out by the liberal Colonel, to the staff and male spectators. Lt. Col. Cendrecourt, the commanding officer of the battalion, did the honors of the pavilion as gracefully and gallantly as he had conducted the operations of the field. He is a fine, soldierly, dashing officer, was well mounted, and looked like a Paladin of old. He was most kind to all the strangers present, and spoke highly of the generous treatment he had himself received when a visitor at Bombay.

The charges of the cavalry were rather amusing, for although the men rode well, and were evidently sturdy, hard-fisted sabreurs, they were mounted on a species of small cart horse, ungainly and clumsy in its movements. The troopers personally are as fine men as can be found among the heavy dragoons of any country.

A day or two before leaving the Mauritius we had witnessed the presentation of colours to the 5th Fusiliers on the Champs de Mars, and thus had an opportunity of contrasting the gallant defenders of the two islands. The men of the 5th are larger, broader, and sturdier looking fellows than the marine battalion of St. Denis, while there is a lightness, elasticity, and wiry look about the latter, indicative of their being tough and troublesome customers in the actual tussle of war. The English soldiers marched more steadily and with a firmer tread than the French, but there was not the same insouciant, intellectual look about the smooth-faced* men of the Fusiliers that was to be seen in the bearded, blue-coated voltigeurs of St. Denis.

* The strange and unaccountable antipathy of the Anglo-Saxon race to the wearing of beards has always appeared to be an absurd and ridiculous weakness in so manly, civilized, and usually sensible a people.

From the absence of that innate politeness and natural good breeding which characterizes most Asiatic and many western nations, the moment an Englishman ventures to show a hirsute countenance in a circle of his fellow-countrymen, the male portion of the assembly begin to button up their breeches pockets and direct the butler to look after the spoons. The conversation of even the gentle sex is apt to glide naturally into commentaries on rat-catchers dogs or badgers. Under a broadside of stares or more palpable demonstrations of disapproval, the unfortunate follower of nature is led to imagine that he has been classed with swindlers, pickpockets, or savages. He may even be tempted to look behind to ascertain if he has a tail, since he has received the treatment of a bear.

A very little reflection on the subject would show that such prejudices are not founded on sound principles, and that the modern male and female costumes of the western world afford far more scope for ridicule and disapproval, than the capillary appendages of chins or lips.

One of the causes of dislike is doubtless due to its being associated with an idea of the absence of personal cleanliness.

Because Cossacks and Tartars and other outside barbarians wear beards and luxuriate in dirt, the practice is deemed to be unclean.

If the argument had the remotest pretension to reason or truth, it would apply with a force proportioned to the increased magnitude of their development, to "the luxuriant locks and fair tresses [which] man's imperial race ensnare." And yet does there exist a barbarian who would desire to see beauty shorn of her greatest ornament, and reduced to the state of 'Jove without his thunder, Venus uncested, or Phoebus unbeamed'!

The smooth shaven scalp of the oily Bráhman, or the martial tuft of the red man of America ought to be the type of propriety in regard to the adornment of the head, if we were only moderately consistent in the matter, and transferred the capillo-phobia from the chin to the crown.

'Tempora mutantur et nos mutamur in illis.' It is not many centuries since the Saxon churl fought for his beard and liberties against the Norman conqueror, and resisted depilatory edicts as tending to insult and effiminacy.

The beard of Sir Thomas More has become a portion of English history, from the care with which he treated it in the closing scene of his life, since *it* "had not committed treason."

Time was when 'twas said and sung with truth of England,

'Tis merry in the hall
When beards wag all.'

From the fourteenth to the sixteenth century the beard was generally worn in England. Who will venture to say that the worthies of that age as transmitted to us in the authentic portraits of the period, or immortalized in the writings of the great dramatist, are unworthy, unmanly or unbecoming representatives of the manliness, intelligence, and even beauty of the Saxon countenance. The race which extorted the celebrated saying of St. Augustin—"*Non Angli sed Angeli forent, si Christiani essent,*" could have had no mean pretensions to the highest order of 'grace of form and comeliness of feature.'

It would be idle to contrast them further—both I doubt not are worthy representatives of the prowess and qualities of their different nations, and would maintain their ancient reputations in well-contested fields. The number of mounted officers in the British corps, with the brightness of the scarlet uniform, give them a somewhat more brilliant appearance than the subdued hue of the French dress affords.

The effective field force of regular troops in Bourbon is said to be about two thousand men, including between one and two hundred stalwart gens d'armes, scattered over the island as a mounted police. There is a considerable force of militia also, but I imagine that their quality is pretty much the same as that of the burgher troops of most countries. They were reviewed by the Governor on the 4th of May, but I was absent at Salazie, and did not witness the ceremony.

The police of Bourbon is organized and conducted on the same effective footing as in France, and consists of mounted gens d'armes and armed gardes champêtres. They are all natives of France, lead a life of much activity and exposure, and are most efficient guardians of the public peace. During our excursions into the country we saw two gangs of run-away coolies, each led by a couple of mounted patrols, and trotting along very discon-

Who would venture to 'mundify the muzzle' of the immortal bard of Avon, or to shave the sturdy barons, who literally as well as figuratively *bearded* king John at Runnymede.

The besetting sin of the Anglo-Saxon race, after all, is conformity. Provided it receives the impress of fashion and is sealed with the signet of the foolish, nothing is too extravagant or ridiculous for adoption.

Those who venture to run counter to the popular prejudice are ranked among the eccentric and absurd. Truly in many matters of common sense, the 'wise conform to the foolish.'

"Few are those who venture even for the shortest time into that hazy world of independent thought, where a man is not upheld by a crowd of other men's opinions, but where he must find a footing of his own. Among the mass of men there is no resistance to conformity. Could the history of opinions be fully written, it would be seen how large a part in human proceedings the love of conformity, or rather the fear of non-conformity has occasioned. It has triumphed over all other fears; over love, hate, pity, sloth, anger, truth, pride, comfort, self-interest, vanity, and maternal love. It has torn down the sense of beauty in the human soul, and set up in its place ugly little idols which it compels us to worship with more than Japanese devotion. It has contradicted nature in the most obvious things, and has been listened to with abject submission. Its empire has been no less extensive than deep-seated. The serf to custom points his finger at the slave to fashion, as if it signified whether it is an old or a new thing which is irrationally conformed to."*

The same sound thinker, close reasoner, and profound philosopher, one who has brought simple truths from the bottom to the surface of the well, and clothed abstruse thoughts in simple garb, has also remarked upon this sin of conformity in dress and fashion, that when he sees an eastern man sweeping by in something flowing and stately, he feels inclined to take off his hat to him (only that he thinks the hat might frighten him) and say 'Here is a great unhatted, uncravated, bearded man, not a creature clipt and twisted and tortured in tailors' hands.'

Of a truth we are of a race who 'quarrel with nature for making us men instead of women,' who rob the face of man of its manliest attributes, who daily and hourly outrage nature and common sense in our strange garbs and unseemly fashions, and yet arrogate to ourselves the office of holding the cynic's lantern to our neighbours.

* Friends in Council, vol. I. p. 23.

solately at a rapid rate. They were fettered together by the wrists and seemed to have a wholesome dread of their conductors, who are said to be very expert in tracing and hunting them out. Their tall glazed caps, long blue cloaks, clanking sabres, and martial air, struck us much as they were riding along in the cold, grey dawn of a wet, dismal morning. When I saw them, I could not help thinking that an active, energetic, mounted and armed patrol in Bengal would be far more effectual in preventing dacoity, and putting a stop to the robbery and murder of native travellers on the road side, than the existing village chowkedaree and burkundauze system.

They should, however, be very differently mounted and equipped, and composed of better materials than were the equestrian Dogberries who distinguished themselves at the reception of the Sikh guns, and are immortalized in the grand cartoon of that memorable event.

The hospitality of Bourbon and Mauritius has long been proverbial, and although most of the older inhabitants of both islands declared that the difficulties, struggles and losses of these interesting colonies had reduced them much from their former palmy state, *we* certainly should not have discovered it.

I mentioned in Port Louis one day my intention to visit the interior, and before the next evening had no fewer than thirty introductions to planters and others in the various places through which I was to pass. To St. Denis I took but one letter, and yet I think it would have been impossible for any one in any quarter of the world, to have experienced more real kindness, and a more thoroughly friendly welcome than I met with in that good town.

We did not exactly find with Felicidus that delicious cakes disputed with equally nice bread, which should enter our mouths first, nor did the fish come to the houses ready fried, yet it proved practically a land flowing with milk and honey, sending us away after a brief sojourn with a multitude of kindly recollections and pleasant memories, that will not readily be forgotten. I had often heard of the munificent open houses of the Merchant Princes of the City of Palaces, when the pagoda tree was neither a fiction nor a mere figure of speech. I had, likewise, not forgotten the account of the wonderful festival of Tremolum, where tempting little pigs ran about the streets ready roasted, yet had I never realized these pleasant fictions so well as in the little spot of the Indian Ocean, which lies within a few miles of the east coast of Madagascar. It should be remembered that this feasting and profusion, and cordial welcome to the stranger, is not practised out of the abundance of the good things of this world, for Bourbon is no El Dorado nor is it a California of hidden treasure. In few places is so much accomplished with such limited means—nowhere is it more practically proved that cheerful contentment is not dependent on length of purse or pride of pocket.

A brief description of one or two of the entertainments to which I refer may not be altogether without interest to the Indian reader, and I hope may tempt others to travel the same unfrequented path. The extension of our social relations cannot but be beneficial to all, and tend to soften down the asperities and trials inseparable from our exile and pilgrimage in this distant land of the Sun.

The first was a dinner given by a barrister of the court, a benedict and master of the masonic lodge at St. Denis. The party consisted of the ladies of his family, and a considerable number of male relations and friends, in all we could not have sat down less than thirty in number. At most of these entertainments it is usual for only the ladies of the household to be present, the rooms are scarcely large enough to admit of more being asked. We all assembled in an outer verandah, and after being kindly and specially introduced to every one present, were summoned to the feast.

The table was covered with a profusion of vivers, every thing from the fish and soup to the dessert being spread before us at once, instead of being brought in separate courses, with long pauses between them, as customary with us. This might possibly have been owing to the paucity of servants ; it was a practice we found to pervade every entertainment at which we assisted. After the soup and side dishes, the fish was handed round, then the turkey and ham, and lastly vegetables in silver dishes, all different from our customs in these matters. The wines were excellent, there being an abundance of claret, madeira, hock, and champagne, beer coming in at the end of the dinner to assist in its digestion. It was no mere 'Dominie's dribble o'drink,' but more good sack than even Jack Falstaff could have pocketed. The whole was most unlike the tedious formality and ennuie of an Indian dinner party.

When the good things had been done ample justice to, commenced the proposal of toasts, also a general practice in Bourbon and at the French houses in the Mauritius. With us, except on special public occasions, it is seldom practised, and when resorted to is generally considered a bore and a wet blanket. Not so with our gayer and more sprightly neighbours. It was so managed as to be an agreeable addition to the pleasures of the entertainment, and to call forth sentiments of kindliness and welcome that we should have been more than barbarians not to have responded to. Our host, from his bar experience, was evidently a practised orator, and delighted us by the happy terms in which he embodied his sentiments. In most countries the members of the legal profession take the lead on such occasions. The best chairmen of public dinners, and the most amusing members of private society, are every where certainly from the Bar.

The dinner over, ladies and gentlemen adjourned together to the drawing-room, when some other friends came in and the room was cleared for a dance, which was kept up with much hilarity until a late hour. Liqueurs, coffee and tea were partaken of during the evening, and our host accompanied us home, thus ending as pleasant an evening as could be spent in any part of the world.

The great breakfasts were exactly on the same scale, and conducted in the same manner as the dinner, with the exception of beginning at eleven in the forenoon, and sometimes lasting until two or three in the afternoon.

In many respects the social habits of the good folks at St. Denis are more sensible and better suited for a tropical climate than are our Indian fashions. The usual family dinner hour is seldom later than six o'clock, and friends are expected to drop in at eight to spend a social evening together, with music, dancing, conversation, and other agreable ways of killing time, without formality, fuss, or parade of dress. No lady is visible before one in the afternoon, and our Bengal siestas seem to be unknown.

The amusements of the lords of the creation are pretty much as with us. In the hotel Joinville, billiards, dominoes, and drinking pale ale appeared to be the order of the day, and of a portion of the night too, with many of the regular frequenters of that establishment. The café at the hotel d'Europe is also a great source of attraction and kept open to a much later hour.

A never-failing source of amusement to most of us, and to an admiring audience of a very miscellaneous description, was the daily drill of the flank companies of the marine battalion, on the Place. After being detached into squads under their respective corporals, and performing with becoming gravity the goose step and similar mysterious methods of making soldiers, the arms were piled and the men turned to gymnastics. This seemed to be a complete pastime to the soldiers, and was full of fun to the spectators. The most popular portion of the proceeding was jumping over a cord, in which many tumbled somersets amidst shouts of laughing from all present. The bearded old pioneers who held the ends of the rope appeared to take a pleasure in elevating it slily and quickly, when some more than ordinarily ambitious hero o'erleap'd himself, coming down quickly on the other side. They were marched on and off with bugles and drums, and were certainly much harder worked than our men are.

There were two fires during our visit, and from the very prompt and efficient manner in which means were taken to extinguish them, I should imagine them to be of frequent occurrence.

As soon as a fire is perceived, the bell of the principal church notifies it at once to the whole town, by three rapid strokes with a brief interval, a tocsin of alarm of which the effect is electrifying.

The drums beat to arms, soldiers from all directions hasten either to the barracks or to the scene of action, and in a very short space of time a body of disciplined men are marched to the spot by beat of drum. Some of these are without arms to act as a fatigue party in working the engines and saving life and property, others are armed to form a cordon to keep off the crowd and to prevent irregularities. The engines are under the charge of a detail of Sappeurs Pompiers, an armed fire brigade, which also makes for the conflagration as fast as the men can drag the machines. Mounted gens d'armes are in movement, and a very few minutes elapse before active, organized, and well-directed exertions are made to arrest the flames. On both occasions to which I refer, the Governor and his staff were among the earliest persons on the ground.

How very different is this from the utter absence of anything like organization or method to effect the same object in the metropolis of British India. Twice have I seen more than two hundred huts utterly destroyed, before a wretched powerless engine was on the spot, or any proper means taken to prevent the extension of the destructive element.

There are, in fact, many things in the philosophy of our excellent neighbours that we might adopt with benefit.

It is doubtless a misnomer to speak of slaves when slavery has ceased to exist, but as the emancipation of the negro population of Bourbon is a very recent event, from the effects of which the island is still suffering, the relics of the old system of bondage are even yet visible. There can be no doubt of the abstract right of every human being to freedom, and of the degrading effects of loss of liberty upon those unfortunate races to whom it is still denied in some parts of the world, yet in carrying out even so philanthropic and proper a measure as general manumission, some share of wisdom and discretion is necessary.

He who has been born in bondage, reared under its blighting influence, and accustomed from his very cradle to be dependent on others, is no more fitted at once for uncontrolled licence, than is the starved man to eat a full meal, or the newly restored eye of the blind to face the bright light of day. They all need a certain stage of careful preparation, to fit them for their new state.

This is abundantly evident in the present condition of a multitude of the ancient slaves both of Bourbon and of the Mauritius. They are naturally an idle, vain, pleasure-loving race, and, with the rare exceptions of those who have received some degree of education, or who are gifted by nature, are unwilling to undergo any greater degree of exertion than is sufficient for immediate maintenance and support. The consequence has been that the majority have become squatters on small patches of land, upon the produce of which they live, in many instances in a state bordering on misery and starvation. Improvidence and want of care for the morrow are producing their inevitable effects, the result of which cannot fail to be crime, disease and their attendant horrors. In the meantime the proprietors have received no compensation, no provision on a sufficiently extended scale has been made for the cultivation of the soil, and a state bordering on general bankruptcy and ruin has been caused to the colony. All this might have been avoided without leaving the stain of slavery to disfigure the fair escutcheon of the young republic.

Most of the old negro race of servants in families have disappeared, and their place seems to be but ill-supplied by the Indian immigrants shipped from the Malabar coast.

The waiters in the hotels are all emancipated half-castes, and a more saucy, idle set of necessary nuisances it would be difficult to discover. Their notions of independence and republican fraternity were not a little absurd and amusing, although they occasionally degenerated into sources of annoyance. They all dub themselves citizens, and strut about very much after the fashion of Sultan Cockaloo in Tom Cringle's Log, being as proud and about as useful, as Paddy's dog with two tails. This was the general rule, there were some exceptions to it.

The sugar plantations are now almost entirely cultivated by coolies from the Malabar coast, or who at least are shipped at Póndicherry. Among these I saw men from the Deccan, Mysore territory, and Carnatic, most, if not all of whom must have been crimped and kidnapped from the British territories. They are well treated, fairly paid, and have not an undue or unhealthy amount of labour to perform. Their fulfilment of the duties involved in their contract is more rigidly exacted than in the Mauritius, and while they are protected from tyranny or ill-treatment, they are made to conduct themselves with propriety and order.

I was unable to ascertain the exact number of Indian labourers on the island. Some accounts raised it as high as 30,000 others fixed it at about 20,000; the latter is, I believe the nearest approximation to the truth.

Wherever I went in the Mauritius I heard complaints of the inadequate power possessed by the planter over his labourers, and of the idleness, impudence, and gross insubordination of the coolies. I had some opportunities of personally witnessing this, and of seeing the state of irritation and ill-feeling produced by it. It is true that the majority of them are the refuse of our Indian labouring population, and some, I suspect, are not altogether unacquainted with jail discipline. It is right that the coolie at a distance from his home and country should be well shielded by the strong arm of the law, but at the same time he should be made to feel that he is not at liberty to have his own way in the disposal of his time and labour. A visitor from India, accustomed to the quiet demeanour and respectful behaviour of servants and labourers in that country, is apt to be surprized at their cool impudence and nonchalance in the Mauritius. They do not hesitate openly to tell their masters that they dare not punish them, and to treat them with an amount of disrespect that would not be tolerated for a moment in their own country.

I was very much tickled with the unblushing effrontery of a gardener in the Savanne district, who, when he heard I was from Hindustan, asked me if the Company's Raj was not knocked in the head. He had heard it said that we had taken the Punjab, but didn't believe it; "in fact," he continued, "My rajah intended to put down the Company, and I dare say he has done so by this time." He turned out to be a native of one of the petty states in the Nerbudda territory, and I left him terribly crestfallen, by informing him in the presence of an admiring gang of fellow-coolies, that his rajah had been recently hanged for sheep stealing! The fact is that the coolie is too well treated in the Mauritius. He is well paid, pampered, and all his complaints are listened to, while his master appears to have little redress against the shortcomings of his immigrant labourers. It is nearly as much for the interest of India, as it is for that of the Mauritius, that a more extended immigration of a better class of tillers of the soil should be encouraged. By its means, much wealth is brought by the coolies to be expended in their own country. They come back more robust, manly, and less prejudiced than when they left their homes, and the influence of their acquired knowledge cannot fail to be useful to their own countrymen.

The contrast between the lean, hungry Cassius-looking coolies who arrive at Port Louis, and the stout, muscular well fed fellows with well lined purses

who leave its shores, is very remarkable, and good proof both of the healthiness of the climate and the excellent treatment they receive.

A few simple regulations regarding the remitting of their money would be very beneficial to them. At present they carry it with them, and not unfrequently about their persons, for additional security. The consequence is that during the voyage they are in a constant state of feverish anxiety regarding its safety, and scarcely ever come up on deck, unless forcibly compelled to do so, to admit of their habitation being scrubbed and ventilated once a week.

The great want at present experienced, is of an adequate number of women of good character to accompany the men. The few who go there are from the lowest and worst class of society; they are a fruitful source of crime and disorder among the men, and are seldom, if ever, really their wives. Again, the expense of carrying them down is much greater than it need be, from the unwisely liberal amount of space granted to each on board the immigrant ships. The quantity given to the sepoy in a transport sent on service, is amply sufficient for every purpose of health and cleanliness, if they are properly cared for on board. To this I can personally testify from having been nearly a month on board a coolie ship, during which time I omitted no opportunity of making myself acquainted with every thing regarding their wants, wishes, and peculiarities.

The whole subject of immigration is at present attracting much attention at the Mauritius, and justly so, for on it depends entirely the prosperity of the island. The Governor is himself an old Indian, and so intimately acquainted with every bearing of the question, that it is to be hoped his wise and experienced counsels will be attended to. He has forgotten none of the kindly ways and generous sentiments that rendered him so justly popular in India, and all visitors from that vast territory are sure of a frank and a hearty welcome to his hospitality. Experto crede!

Among the subjects in Bourbon that most strike a visitor from Bengal, are the large number of officers employed in every department of the state, civil and military, and the very low scale of salaries, such as to be certainly incompatible with the well being and dignity, particularly of the higher officers. The pay of the Governor is not half that of the Secretary to the Government of Bengal; the salary of the Chief Justice of the Supreme Court in Calcutta is greater than that of the whole thirteen judges of the Court of appeal in St. Denis together; and the allowances of the military and civil departments are barely sufficient for the maintenance of the mere externals of rank and position.

The chief medical officer of the island, who enjoys the rank of Colonel, has served for more than thirty years with distinction, and was ten years ago deemed deserving of the distinction of the cross of the Legion of Honour, receives a lower salary than the junior assistant surgeon in the Company's army in charge of a regiment. M. Dauvin is a man of great ability and experience, and can rise very little higher in his own service and department.

So far as I could ascertain, nearly all the government employés, at any rate those holding offices of trust and importance, are either natives of France or brought up in Europe. I met with only one exception, but he is a man of energy of character and ability, such as would have commanded success any where.

SALAZIE.

Most persons are aware that there are in Bourbon mineral springs of great value and efficacy, but, beyond the bare fact of their existence, little or nothing is known to us about them. It appears that an analysis of the mineral waters of the island was published in the Indian newspapers some time ago. I have never seen it, nor has it made much impression on the public mind, since the visits of invalids from Hindustan have been so rare as to be almost unknown to the present generation of inhabitants. At intervals an occasional wanderer from the Mauritius has found his way across, and there is a mythical legend extant in the mountains of a 'milor Anglais' who rode up from the Escalier to the Source, and created an intense sensation among the Maidens of the Mist. His noble steed and martial air are well remembered, as well as his entire devotion to the care of his charger. Like the renowned Dugald Dalgetty, his Gustavus seems to have been his first and greatest anxiety, and he is said to have quitted the healing waters the morning after his arrival, solely because he could not find fitting accommodation for the companion of his travels. All this was told us by a bright-eyed damsel, who must then have been a bare-footed little lassie, too young to attract the notice of a gay and dashing cavalier. I afterwards ascertained that the illustrious stranger was a field officer in the Bengal cavalry, whose liberality and exploits in the island have left a lasting impression. One denizen of our ditch is also spoken of, his patriarchal beard and pilgrim's mien, with his known scientific acquirements and pleasing address, having produced nearly as durable an interest as the gallant bearing of the Troubadour.

At three o'clock in the morning of Friday the 2nd of May, our small party started for Salazie. The dinner of our excellent friend the barrister had kept us up until the witching hour of one, so that we were not in very brilliant trim for a mountain trip. It was as dark as pitch when we set forth and the gloom of the yet unborn day was increased by a succession of drizzling showers, thick and fine as the cold gray mantle of a highland mist. We had hired a carriage with an English coachman, to take us to the foot of the pass, where we were to find means to carry us to the fountain-head.

The first part of the road was scarcely discernible, and we were only conscious of a succession of hills and dales, with an occasional bridge, until, through a long avenue of trees, the brilliant light of St. Suzanne appeared like a bright beacon to guide us on our way. A little beyond, just as the gray dawn was peeping, we changed horses, our Jehu plunging through a field of sugar-cane, and disappearing for nearly half an hour, before the relay made its appearance.

While thus occupied, strolling along the roadside and snuffing the first breath of the fine morning air, a couple of mounted dragoons passed us, driving a string of captive coolies before them. The distant sound of the horses hoofs ringing upon the hard road, and the clanking of the horsemen's sabres long before they emerged from the gloom, brought strongly to my recollection a little adventure that I happened to witness in Normandy some twenty years ago. I was travelling alone from Paris and was in the interior of the diligence with two nuns, who were telling their beads with much devotion, when near the bottom of a steep hill, the axle-tree broke, the huge lumbering machine swung off the road with a sudden jerk, and came down with an awful crash into a large ditch, bordering an extensive vineyard. The number of passengers was small, and all were extracted without much damage, when we assembled, somewhat a disconsolate crew, looking at the wreck of our vessel.

The ropes were cut and all the horses released, except one poor wheeler, who lay crushed under the carriage which had rolled upon him. The postillion was whistling a favorite air from Robert le Diable, which had recently appeared in Paris, and we were wondering how to get extricated from our difficulty, when the Conducteur sounded a few shrill notes upon a bugle hanging round his neck.

In a few moments we heard the clear ringing sounds of a horse's feet urged to a smart canter with the rattling of a horseman's accoutrements, along the road we had just passed without seeing any sign of life or animation. Almost simultaneously similar sounds were heard in two other directions, and in a marvellously brief space of time, emerging from the darkness like the mounted heroes of old romances, some five gens d'armes armed to the teeth were on the spot. With their aid, assistance was procured from a neighbouring village, the axle mended, the dead horse cast into a ditch, and we were once more lumbering on our way, with a profound conviction of the vigilance and efficiency of the French rural patroles.

At six o'clock we reached the village of St. Andrè, near the Rivière du Mat, where we had been advised to breakfast and remain. The shops were just beginning to open when we descended at a miscellaneous store that supplied everything, from covering for the body to the means of lining its interior. Here, after a delay of nearly two hours we were set down to the toughest and dirtiest meal I ever assisted in the disposal of. I thought that it was impossible to find on the surface of the globe more desperate exercise for the teeth than was afforded by the tenacious beef and mutton of the Kandian province of Ceylon. But I was mistaken. The patriarchal cock of St. Andrè, who must have announced the return of dawn to at least three generations of long-lived inhabitants, was roasted for our entertainment. To make any impression on his iron sides was a physical impossibility, abandoned in despair by the whole of our party. Christopher North speaks of having once assisted at the dissection of a cock "boiled down in his tough antiquity to a tatter." Not even a Papin's digester could have softened him of St. Andrè.

For this unsavory apology for a meal we paid a dollar a head, besides losing two of the pleasantest hours of the day. Travellers, in future, beware of St. Andrè, and carry your own breakfast with you, if you be wise and willing to profit by our experience!

Among the idle crew hanging about the place was a sturdy, impudent, Massanielo-looking fellow, with bare legs and a true lazzaroni air of swagger and independence about him. We hired him to carry our baggage up the pass, and make himself generally useful, which he certainly did, for he was an amusing varlet, who waited on us at dinner, dried our raiments, and coolly drank our healths in the remains of each unfinished bottle of wine at table.

Sundry scraggy, miserable, starved and most wretched Rosinantes were brought out to carry us up the pass, but we preferred trusting to our natural means of locomotion, the more especially as the value attached to these ghostly quadrupeds was preposterous.

At the Rivière du Mat the road to Salazie turns off at right angles, running like the radius of a circle towards the centre of the isle. It very soon becomes picturesque, and after winding round the shoulder of a hill takes the traveller into a deep valley, along the bed of which, stony and rough, runs the river. The hills on the sides of this ravine are lofty and covered with forest trees nearly to their summits. In some places the spray of tiny waterfalls sprinkles the passer by, where they form small, bubbling, murmuring streams, running across the road. The scenery gradually becomes grander and more silent and solitary in character, the ravines look darker, more abrupt and precipitous, and the cascades become more numerous and grander in appearance, until the Escalier, or foot of the great ravine, is reached.

About a mile from this, on the left hand side, an unusually rugged, romantic ravine branches off, with a lofty cataract descending its steep rocky side, like a compact stream of molten silver. In this chasm a runaway slave once concealed himself successfully for four years, living upon roots and fruits, and the produce of a little Indian corn, which he took with him and planted. It seems almost inaccessible to anything less agile and sure-footed than a chamois, and nothing can be imagined more bare, gloomy, and unpromising than the entrance of this dark and dismal gorge.

At the Escalier the carriage road ceases abruptly, and the broad valley is passed by a wooden bridge, to which they were building at the time of our visit, solid, massive stone piers.

At the other side begins a foot or bridle-path, which following very much the natural levels of the sides of the ravine, ascends to the source of the mineral waters, at the foot of the great mountain called the Snowy Peak. During its course up the valley for twelve or thirteen miles, as we conjectured the distance to be, it sometimes rises suddenly and winds in a zig-zag form round hills, the character of the scenery varying with every turn.

Although it rained heavily for a considerable part of our ascent, and we laboured along with some difficulty, nothing could damp our enjoyment of the magnificent prospects, scattered in profusion on every side. The cataracts rushing down the hill sides were plentiful as blackberries in a bramble hedge, and some of them extremely beautiful, although none were on a very large scale. In some places whole sides of the hills had been torn down by the hurricanes, and cast into the deep abyss ; in other situations our path overhung stupendous precipices, also leading to the eternal rocky bottom, along which the stream was brawling, now leaping with sullen roar and spotless foam over large boulders of rock, and again murmuring with musical sound, clear as crystal and cold as charity, over a smooth, pebbly surface.

It has often been remarked that it is impossible to describe scenery so as to enable fireside travellers to realize any definite and accurate notion of its real characters. I believe this to be true ; and although the Salazie valley does not possess the magnificent grandeur of the Alpine passes, and its waterfalls are little more than silver threads upon a sable ground, it has a beauty and interest of its own that more than repay the pains and fatigues of its ascent.

Between the Escalier and the Source we passed two or three pretty bridges, constructed with much strength and ingenuity, with cross and supporting beams, something on the principle of wooden piers at French watering places. To the site of one of them, thrown over an ugly chasm in a rock with steep, perpendicular sides, and a fall of at least an hundred feet into a boiling stream beneath, a small legend is attached. A run-a-way slave pursued and brought to bay, jumped boldly over the precipice, plunged into the roaring pool, and escaped unhurt, as he deserved to do, after a feat of so much dar-

ing, and so irresistible a desire for liberty. It almost made me giddy even to look down upon it, behind the protection of a stout parapet.

In several places the valley becomes broad, and forms little plateaus on the sides, which are inhabited and cultivated by the negroes recently freed from slavery. A few of these were fertile-looking spots, and had an air of careful, successful husbandry about them delightful to witness; the sugar-cane, maize and vegetable gardens being neat, trim, and flourishing.

In a few places we saw coffee apparently wild, for the bushes were long, straggling, and untrimmed, the berry small and scattered, very unlike the Contractor's field at Rathongodde, or the better quality of coffee grown on other estates in the province of Kandy. We traced the coffee plants to an elevation of nearly 4000 feet, and it was curious to find in it here the same loathsome *bug* which is a source of so much loss and vexation to the Ceylon planter.

One of the greatest sources of pleasure in the pass, was the number and beauty of the wild flowers and plants growing in endless profusion at the road side. The wild raspberry, honey-suckle, rose and violet, with multitudes of beautiful convolvuluses, and at least twenty different species of fern, literally strewed our path. Pretty and rare butterflies lent their gorgeous colours to heighten the glories of the scene, and enormous spiders had woven their fairy webs across the way.

The scenery in some parts strongly reminded me of my recent wanderings through the picturesque valleys, and lofty ridges of the central province of Ceylon. Upon the whole the greater seeming loftiness of the mountains gave a grander effect to Salazie, but the hand of man had done less to bring out the beauties of nature, than in the stupendous monuments of engineering skill exhibited in the Karraganava and Ramboddie passes. The forests clothing the sides and summits of the Kandian hills are denser, the trees larger, and the thousand tints of the foliage from bright scarlet to every shade of green and brown, more striking than in the Bourbon woods. From not having scaled the crest of the snowy ridge, I am unable to say whether the coup d'œil of the whole island gained from that lofty pinnacle is finer than the corresponding view from the pinnacle of Pedro Tallagalla, above the plain of Newera Ellia. With all its undoubted claims to grandeur and the picturesque, I must confess, that I saw nothing in the coast scenery of Reunion that pleased me so much as the enchanting view of Mahébourg from the ruins of the old town of Grandport in the Mauritius, nor was there a valley that the eye scanned with such thorough enjoyment as the glorious Maturata valley seen from the ridge of Yakabendy Kellie, or the quiet character and rural beauty of the Hewahetti range, viewed from the Swiss cottage at Rathongodde in Ceylon.

The hardy rhododendron which imparts an almost magical effect to the wild scenery of the Kandian ridges from the brilliancy of its scarlet flowers, where all else is naked and barren, I did not find in our way to Salazie. It must be confessed, however, that we did not see the grandest, most fantastic and striking portions of the Bourbon scenery, which are said to afford endless views of the wildest, most sombre, and romantic description. This I can readily believe from the physical character of the portion we travelled over. The geological formation of the island is undoubtedly volcanic, there being still one active volcano on its surface, besides some craters which have most likely become dormant during the current geological era. Its rocks and mountains are basaltic, and limestone only exists in the coral reefs bounding its inaccessible coast.

Nearly midway between the Escalier and the Source, is a large village, having a church, a Mayoralty, and several substantial houses, besides being the head-quarters of the commissary of police of the district. Here we halted for half an hour, and became acquainted with the Mayor and the Commissary, the former a strong, hale, rosy-faced old man, with much more of a Saxon than a Gallic look, the latter an obliging active man, who is the proprietor of the pavilions at the watering place. He sent on a messenger to announce our approach to his wife, the busy, bustling manager of the sparkling spring.

The village is built on the largest of the natural plateaus we saw, and is a truly lovely spot.

At four in the afternoon, although we had strolled along leisurely, we reached the Salazie itself, not a little tired by our wet and weary walk.

Madame Cazeau, with the aid of her black-eyed daughter, soon arranged a pavilion for our accommodation, in which the travel stains of the road were rapidly removed. We then descended along a steep, winding path, as pretty and picturesque as any we had passed in coming up, and at length reached the 'Source,' as the issue of the mineral spring is termed.

In a small, circular and somewhat dilapidated summer-house, we found a gay party of ladies assembled, one in complete Swiss costume, which not only accorded well with the surrounding scenery, but exhibited as symmetrical a figure, and unexceptionable a foot and ancle, as any lover of the sublime and beautiful could desire. In front of this fairy bower, and beneath it a clear, limpid, sparkling jet of water was rising from a narrow pipe. On a small ledge near it were a couple of tumblers, and beneath it a little excavation in the ground coated with the ferruginous looking deposit of the medicated streams. Here the pilgrims drink the waters, and talk over the various topics of interest that arise in the restricted circle of a knot of valetudinarians.

The water is bright, clear, sparkling, and tastes not unlike tepid soda water: if anything, however, it is more palatable and pungent with the smallest possible soupçon of a ferruginous flavour. It has more than once been analyzed with care and skill, so that its properties and constituents are well known. The most careful and trustworthy examination is that of an able and excellent Chemist, Monsr. Marcadieu, to whose kindness I am indebted for the result of his investigations carried on at the Source itself. It is contained in a subsequent portion of this sketch.

So far as the limited means at my disposal permitted I verified the accuracy of Monsr. Marcadieu's examination. The ordinary amount taken by a moderate consumer is six or eight glasses during the day, beginning at an early hour of the morning. Some went as far as twenty-two tumblers in the same space of time, with benefit, and without nausea or sickness. The large excess of free carbonic acid present, renders palatable what would otherwise be a disagreeable draught.

The climate of Salazie is so invigorating, that what would elsewhere be deemed unbearable discomforts, are submitted to without inconvenience or complaint. Still there is strong room for improvement, in the rude comfortless shanties constructed for the convenience of visitors.

They are at present as primitive as the log houses of the backwoods of America, and deficient in the thousand and one cheap little contrivances to which the English in particular attach so much importance as ministering to comfort and contentment.

Some of them are prettily perched on romantic nooks like eyrie's nests on the hill side, and the daily climbing up and down to the central point of gathering, affords a fair amount of active exercise in the open air.

The little station is beautifully situated. It appears to form the flat bottom of a semicircle of lofty hills, covered with forest trees, with the exception of the Piton des Neiges, which towers up into the clouds, bold, barren, dark, and unclothed with the remotest trace of verdure or vegetable life. There are many accessible and agreeable strolls in its vicinity, that to a sociable, enterprizing band would be the very paradise of picnics. Even the summit of the Snowy range is practicable for ladies, and the view from the crest is said to be magnificent. It there forms a broad ledge of table-land, from which Cilaos range may readily be reached. It was my intention to have undertaken this trip, but the limited duration of my leave, and the uncertainty of finding my way back to Calcutta within the prescribed limits, prevented my accomplishing this, and one or two other excursions that I would gladly have made. The Cilaos station is more wild, primitive, and inaccessible than Salazie. The waters are more abundant, and richer in mineral ingredients. An extemporaneous bath may there be formed at any moment by scraping out a hollow in the sand. I regret much that I did not see it.

At six o'clock we were summoned to the cleanest and most tempting repast that we had seen, away from the amenities of private life in the large towns. A magnificent, tasty turkey, excellent vegetables, capital bread, and the whitest of napery, formed a banquet for a Sybarite to which we hungry travellers did ample justice. The wines were fair, and we all fell in love with Madame Cazeau, her fair daughter, and their unexceptionable housewifery.

The accommodation was scanty, but neat, and likewise of the cleanest, priceless boons to those accustomed to the prodigal cleanliness of an Indian home.

Should other pilgrims in search of that greatest of all blessings, health, be tempted to wend their way to Salazie, Madame Cazeau will receive and accommodate them on the following terms, a literal translation of a memorandum which she gave me at my request :—

" Madame Cazeau of Salazie will receive invalids from India on the following terms :—

" Board and lodging for grown up persons, eight rupees a day, children from four to twelve years of age, three rupees.

" The table will always be liberally supplied—the wine of good quality; half draught and half bottled—Champagne twice a week, at the rate of a bottle for four persons.

" Medicines extra.

Means of transport.

" An arm chair (tonjon) with six bearers from the Escalier to the Source fourteen rupees. Ponies, mules, or donkeys, six rupees. Luggage porters, two rupees, or a dollar for every fifty pounds weight.

" When a family is numerous a reduction will be made, especially if an expensive table is not required. The table will be served exactly as for the English visitors in May, 1851."

Turkeys and poultry with nice bread, and an abundance of excellent vegetables are the staple articles of consumption. Beef and mutton are of course out of the question, unless taken up at considerable expense. A diligence leaves St. Denis for St. Andrè twice every day, and at all times, the Source can be reached without distress or inconvenience in twelve hours.

The height of the mineral springs at Salazie is 872 mêtres, or 2616 French feet, which are equal to about 2861 English feet.

Those of Cilaos are 3343 French or 3655 English feet in elevation. This, with the latitude of the island, rather more than twenty degrees to the Southward of the Equator, will give a tolerably good idea of the mean temperature of those delighful spots. The variation in the range of the thermometer during the twenty-four hours is not so great as at Newera Ellia, the celebrated Ceylon Sanatarium, and the climate is quite as cold, if not colder, notwithstanding that the Cingalese plain is six thousand feet above the level of the ocean. On the whole, with the undoubted efficacy and value of its mineral waters, I prefer Salazie as a Sanatarium to any place in the East with which I am acquainted, and for the permanent cure of many Indian

diseases, I am convinced that it must be far superior to even the healing and genial climate of the Cape. It has the greater advantage of a shorter and less expensive sea voyage, with equally pure air, and mineral treasures which the other does not possess. It is a new country to the Indian resident, has many claims peculiar to itself, and none will, I am convinced, regret a visit to its hospitable inhabitants.

It was originally my intention to have returned to St. Denis on the day succeeding our arrival at Salazie, in order to witness the interesting ceremonies of the fête of the Republic. Upon arriving at the Source, however, I heard that a young man was dying in a neighbouring pavilion, and all the little community of Salazie were much interested in his fate. At the request of the gentlemen present, on learning that I was a medical man, I went to see the poor fellow and found him nearly moribund. He was so far gone as to be perfectly insensible, and although I felt that human means could not then snatch him from the grave, I deemed it my duty to stay, and afford him such little assistance as the almost entire absence of any medical means enabled me to give. I accordingly remained with him until his spirit departed, gently and without a sigh, early on the 4th of May. The expected event occurred at five in the morning and directly all was over I left the pavilion to breathe for a few moments the pure mountain air. Within, all was sad and silent; without, the never-ceasing sullen roar of the stream, the dark shadow of the neighbouring hills, and the effect produced by a young May Moon,

> " Beautiful as if she came,
> Fresh from the Elysian bowers below"

produced a solemnity and touching depth of effect, that I never before experienced in such intensity. He was a handsome young man, in the prime of life, gifted with all that fortune could bestow, and had left a young wife, with a child whom he had never seen, in France. There was much of melancholy attached to his untoward fate, the result of an act of imprudence.

At 10 o'clock, with a bright sun shining above, the air blowing fresh and sweet, the mountain ridges gilded with the bright rays of the glorious luminary of day, and all nature smiling, we set off on our return to St. Denis.

There was something very touching in the whole scene. The body was borne on the shoulders of stout mountaineers, followed by a faithful friend of the deceased gentleman. It was Sunday, and the whole population of the valley, some two or three thousand in number, were returning from Church, in their gay holiday garb. Each turn of the winding path showed picturesque groups, walking in Indian file along the steep ascents, imparting a lively and animated character to the prospect. As glimpses of these groups were discovered from time to time, drawn up at the road-side, and saluting the dead in the simple and touching manner of all Catholics, I thought that I had seldom witnessed anything more affecting, and imparting so poetical a character to the grandeur and beauty of the landscape.

At the Escalier, while waiting for the horses to be harnessed, a pretty, barefooted French woman with a young infant in her arms, came up to me and in a strong Norman accent, long since familiar, entreated that I would visit her husband at that moment lying sick in a neighbouring hut. He was a petty chief of the rural police, and in the exposure of his arduous duties had that morning been attacked with fever. She told me her simple little history on the road, and sighed when she spoke of her "belle Normandie" as having little hope of ever again seeing it. Her husband was a tall, stout, handsome Norman, with all the physical characters of that fine race strongly stamped upon him. He was rolled up in blankets in a raging fever, but as quiet and resigned as a sick child. I gave him the little medicine my fellow-traveller had with him, and then left, perhaps for ever, the Salazie. The occurrences of this day, in the hands of the gifted and charming author of 'High Ways and Bye Ways,' would have furnished materials for one of his most interesting chapters.

We reached St. Denis at dusk, just in time to witness the grand display of fireworks on the Place du Government, concluding the ceremonies of the anniversary which had that day been celebrated. The great square was densely crowded with spectators, the fine military band sent forth its inspiring sounds, and all was redolent of life and enjoyment. The contrast between the event of the morning and the occurrences of the evening, sent me to my pillow musing and meditating upon the strange vicissitudes of human life, and the stern practical lessons to be deduced from a right interpretation of its chequered events.

THE RETURN.

For several days before our departure from St. Denis all communication between the shipping and the shore was cut off. This, although common in the hurricane months, is said to be extremely rare in May. The upper windows of the Hotel de Joinville commanded a fine view of the roadstead. From these we could daily witness the rolling of the vessels in the long, heavy swell, that almost immediately afterwards broke upon the stony strand, with loud and angry roar, curling into huge-crested billows, mantled with foam. The ships rolled so much as occasionally nearly to show their keels, and no boat could have stemmed the surging waves. All this time the flag of interdict was flying, and business apparently at a stand-still. Many an anxious glance was cast around the horizon, and every cloud watched with an interest known only to those who have experienced the destructive blasts of Æolus in this stormy latitude. The mighty effects of the tornado we had already witnessed in the Salazie valley. Many are the tales told of the wild havoc of hurricanes in these islands. Some would seem fabulous did they not leave behind undeniable traces of their irresistible course. During our stay in the island the repairs of the massive stone-wall of the basin adjoining the pier were going on. The sea in March last had effected wide breaches in its apparently impregnable sides. The man on one of the signal hills in the Mauritius, with his house and all pertaining to him, are said to have been blown away, without a vestige being ever seen again. The sudden effect upon the mountain streams is sometimes almost magical. The water rolls down like a massive wall carrying all before it, and comes with such speed as scarcely to permit the people washing clothes in the stream, to escape with life and limb. Human beings and cattle have often been drowned on these occasions. The same is seen in all mountainous tropical regions. The rivers in the province of Kandy are sometimes impassable in an equally short space of time. At one moment clear, fordable, and scarcely ankle-deep; directly afterwards a deep roaring torrent, with huge stones and trunks of trees hurtling together in its troubled race.

The scenes of this elemental strife often reminded me of the graphic account in Tom Cringle's Log, of the tornado in Cuba.

At length, on the 9th of May, the flag-staff intimated that boats might put off, but with great caution, the sea being still heavy and dangerous.

A Marseilles vessel was that day to sail for Calcutta, and as I was anxious to return quickly, I resolved to go on board to see her accommodations. This I found no easy task. At the end of the pier, some twenty feet from the surface of the water, hung a movable rope ladder, the only means of embarkation available, for the violence of the swell would have carried away the wooden ladder had it been lowered for a moment. A pilot was on duty to regulate the intercourse, and to see that no precautions for the prevention of accidents were neglected. All boats were compelled to anchor or be at their oars a few yards beyond the swell, and to approach the pier one at a time as they were wanted. As soon as they were near enough, the person intending to embark descended this Jacob's ladder, and dropped into the boats when they came directly beneath. To a landsman this suspension in mid-air, with the oscillation of the rope and the dark heaving surge beneath, was anything but pleasant. I somewhat miscalculated my time, and tumbled some six feet into the little bark, nearly breaking the arm of one of the rowers, and tearing the flesh of one of my own fingers from the bone. The ship was half a mile off, but as I did not like her accommodations I returned to the shore, glad to find myself once more on *terra firma*.

I remained for some time on the pier watching the process of shipping baggage and cargo, and of filling the water casks of the ships. Nothing can exceed the care of the French authorities in superintending all these operations. The boat loading was anchored at a fixed mooring, some fifty yards beyond the pier head. As soon as a lull occurred in the rolling of the waves, generally after every third swell, the boat was rapidly brought under the pier, and the box, bag, or basket let down by a stout rope. Directly the heavy waves were again seen to approach, the boat was quickly warped away to the kedge, beyond their reach, and this was repeated until the cargo was shipped, when it was smartly rowed off, the line being made over to the next boat in waiting. All this was conducted quickly, systematically, and with such success that I did not see a single package wetted or injured. The same care prevents the loss of life; indeed, I believe, that accidents seldom or never occur. An unfortunate wight who missed his hold would stand but little chance of escaping, as the place abounds in hungry sharks. If he gave them the slip, he would most probably be killed by the violence with which the surf breaks on the shingle beach. Were this soft, shelving, and sandy as at Madras, massulah boats would probably have been used there, but nothing made of wood or iron, I fancy, could be stranded with safety on that iron-bound shore.

The water casks were filled through a hose with a metal mouth-piece screwed on to the end of a large iron pipe running along the barrachois, the height from which the water comes forcing it with facility to the lower level.

At three in the afternoon our party went through the ordeal mentioned above in embarking on the Eglé, and some were suspended, like the Prophet's tomb, rather longer than was safe or pleasant.

Most, if not all, of us parted from the hospitable island with regret, yet in pushing off we gave the friends we left behind us three hearty, honest, English cheers.

The absence of a good harbour, the vast proportion of the land incapable of culture, and the prejudicial influence of the sudden abolition of slavery before any proper provision had been made to replace its compulsory labour, have seriously affected the prosperity of Reunion.

The chief article of export is sugar, and to its cultivation, as in the Mauritius, everything has been sacrificed. The red cane is now universally grown, in consequence of the richer white variety having become liable to a destructive blight, that threatened the very existence of the plant itself, almost as much as the potato was destroyed in Ireland, or the rye plant in some of the epidemic visitations of ergotic disease, that attacked it in the marshy districts of France.

A mixed commission of scientific and practical men was appointed by the Mauritius Government to investigate the subject, to ascertain the cause of the blight, and if possible to suggest remedies for its removal. Their report is an able and interesting document, but leaves the knowledge of the cause of the disease pretty much as it found it.

My own opinion of the matter—if one practically ignorant of the subject, beyond having witnessed its destructive influence, be permitted to entertain or enunciate any notions regarding it—inclines me to think, that, like some epidemic diseases, it will be found to be dependent upon the rapid germination of a low form of vegetable fungus. The cure, I imagine, will be discovered to be some chemical agent that will so act upon the soil in which the plant grows, as to prevent its formation. The incinerated ashes of the diseased canes should be carefully analyzed, as well as the soil in which they grow, and this compared with the results of a like process upon the healthy cane and its soil. The differences, if any, found to exist between them, may give a clue to the origin of the evil.

The arguments in favor of the animalcular nature of these diseases are also very strong, and the application of the microscope to their investigation would seem to strengthen them so much, as in the opinion of many eminent scientific observers, to amount to absolute proof.

In the meantime I would venture to suggest both to those interested in the cane disease, and to the coffee planters in Ceylon, who are as much tormented by the bug, to send home the diseased plants, seeds, &c. to the Epidemiological Society recently formed in London. It ranks among its members some of the most distinguished men of the age, and the most approved means of investigation possessed by modern science would at once be brought to bear upon the subject.

The epidemic diseases of plants bear so remarkable a resemblance in many of their effects to those of animals, that the elucidation of the mysteries of the one, cannot fail to throw some degree of light upon the obscurities of the other. Their joint examination may very possibly lead to valuable discoveries, even to their removal or neutralization by some means analogous to the immortal process of Jenner.

Vanille and coffee are also grown in Bourbon, but not to any great extent, so far as I could ascertain.

There is an absence of commercial life and energy in St. Denis which would almost lead one to believe that it is a declining town, yet, such is probably, not the case. It partakes more in appearance of the *dolce far niente* of the Italians, than of the steady, resolute, unbending energy of the British mercantile world, or of the shrewd, go-a-head, guessing and calculating quality of the Americans. It is not improbable that the adoption, at some future day, of Free-trade principles by the French Republic, may give it an accelerative impulse, and rescue it from ruin, or from what is nearly allied to it, becoming a burthen instead of an assistance, to the mother-country. Be that as it may I am convinced that no Englishman will visit it without receiving the kindest of welcomes, and that none will quit it without the most friendly of feelings towards its enlightened, sociable, and liberal inhabitants.

Our return in the Eglé was infinitely more agreeable than our passage in the Prince Albert. Captain LeClair did all that man could do to add to our comfort, sailed his vessel like an accomplished and able seaman as he is, and in fact united the manly frankness of the English naval officer, with the proverbial urbanity and politeness of his own country. It was blowing half a gale of wind, and the waves were high on the passage, yet, the mid-day of the morrow brought us in sight of 'la belle Maurice,' where we cast anchor early on the morning of the 11th of May. And thus ended our tour to REUNION. Reader! if it please you one-tenth as much in the perusal, as it did me in the performance, I shall have no reason to regret the publication of my '*Rough Notes*.'

STATISTICS OF REUNION.

It was originally my intention simply to have appended to the notes of my personal observations in Bourbon, an analysis of the mineral waters of Salazie and Silhaos, with a few remarks on the tropical diseases for the removal of the effects of which they seem to be suitable.

I find, however, that so little is known regarding this interesting island, which will, I believe, ere long become more frequently visited by pilgrims from India in search of health, that I have departed from my first resolve and thrown together a few details respecting its geography and statistics, which, I trust, will not be found altogether uninteresting.

The information, now, to the best of my belief, first made known to English readers, is chiefly derived from an extremely able report drawn up in 1828 by a M. Thomas, who held a high and important office in the island, and whose remarks and details, I was informed, are as accurate as they are interesting and carefully digested. So far as I had the means of judging, little, if any, radical change can have occurred in the island during the last twenty years, and with the exception of the emancipation of the slave population, the change of government, and a general commercial depression, the Bourbon of 1828 differs little in essentials from the Reunion of 1851.

Like the greater number of the islands in the Indian Seas and the Pacific Ocean, it is essentially a volcanic production. If sufficient evidence of this were not furnished by the peculiar character of its mountains, the abrupt and gigantic fissures which separate them, and the structure of its framework, it would be found in the beds of lava of different thickness and nature which are found every where. To crown all, extinct craters filled with pozzuolana, more or less abundant, and of different eras, are seen in numberless situations on the northern aspect of the island, while there is still in existence an active volcano at its southern extremity.

The hills and mountain peaks which impress their peculiar characters on the physical aspect of the land have all been formed, at different times, by volcanic eruptions, of which the long extinguished fires have left ineffaceable traces of their existence to the north.

The middle of the isle, as if unable to resist their action, appears to have settled down, forming a vast basin at its centre, leaving portions of its solid crust standing erect and abrupt. The chief of these hills are the heights of the River of Rocks and the peak of Langevin, the culminating point of the plaine des Chicots, the partition of St. Stephen's River, Cimandef, the great Bénard, which like a perpendicular wall closes the leeward side of this cavity, and in the midst of this mass of ruins, nearly ten thousand feet above the level of the ocean, the great Snowy Peak.

To judge from the natural slope of the lands surrounding it, it must have been the central and culminating point of the original mountain, as their gradual inclination prolonged from the sea shore would have met either at this peak, or a little above the actual level of its summit.

The great fissures in the sides of the hill which give issue to the waters of the interior, and form the beds of the rivers and the ravines now seen, have all undoubtedly resulted from its disruption.

On the northern side of the island the evidences scattered in every direction, are of extinct volcanic action.

At its southern extremity the volcanic fires are still active, and the surrounding country is a perfect type of utter desolation, without the remotest trace of life or vegetation. The surface is covered with scoriæ, traversed by fissures which open during the succussions of the mountain, when the traveller is stopped by streams of burning lava. The volcano constantly emits clouds of smoke, occasionally sends forth brilliant bursts of flame, and sometimes discharges streams of lava.

The period and direction of the eruptions are irregular; they generally last with greater or less intensity during four months of the year, their activity being somewhat dependent on the state of the atmosphere.

Storms and hurricanes are said to be almost always preceded, at long intervals of time, by eruptions.

The actual orifice of the crater changes nearly every year, shifting over an extent of about two leagues, at probably a distance of three leagues from the border of the sea.

The whole of the intermediate space is covered with the lava of the numerous eruptions which have succeeded each other for many years. The summit of the existing point of eruption is conjectured to be about eleven hundred toises, or, according to the statement in Johnstone's Physical Atlas, 8236 feet above the level of the sea. New and approaching eruptions are announced by the formation of fresh peaks on the crest of the burning ridge; they generally open on the sea aspect of the hill.

The quantity of lava discharged is considerable, and from sinuosities on the surface, the interruption caused by fissures in its course, and other obstructions, the burning stream is frequently a month in reaching the ocean, sometimes in one compact current, occasionally in many branching streamlets.

The phenomena connected with the hardening of its surface and its behaviour generally, are exactly the same as those of other volcanoes. The jet of flame is less in volume than that of Etna or Vesuvius but, quite as lofty, and, except during the eruption of 1812, is seldom accompanied by a shower of ashes.

The geological considerations connected with the formation of the soil, and the gradual production of vegetation from the mosses of the summits of the mountains to the great forests at their bases, although curious and striking to witness, are scarcely of sufficient interest to detail in so very cursory a sketch as this is intended to be.

The soil is separated into three distinct belts or regions, of which one is absolutely barren and uncultivated; a great part of the second cannot be cleared for cultivation, and is most important in regulating the moisture essential for vegetation; the third is peopled and cultivated, and on its fertility depends the prosperity of the island.

The meteorology of Reunion is probably the most important of its physical characters to us, for on the mildness of the climate, the limited range of its variations of temperature, and the extreme purity of its atmosphere depend, in a great measure, its high recommendations as a Sanatarium for tropical invalids.

When to these is added the inestimable value of its mineral waters, as I shall attempt to shew hereafter, I am strongly inclined to regard it as the most eligible asylum and refuge within the tropics, for the victims of some of the most frequent and destructive plagues and pestilences of India.

Placed in a singularly favorable position, between the Cape of Good Hope where the winds blow alternately from East to West at fixed periods, and India where the monsoons are also periodically felt, sheltered on its western aspect by the great island of Madagascar, and to the eastward by the isle of France, Bourbon is not exposed to the full force of either the trades or the monsoons. The temperature of Reunion is always mild and agreeable; its atmosphere is constantly refreshed by a sea breeze, which, blowing during the day, is succeeded by the land wind at night. When the sun is near the winter solstice the highest mountains are covered with snow, and fires are both agreeable and necessary in the neighbouring habitations.

The length of the days varies no more than two hours and a half, the longest day being thirteen hours and sixteen minutes, and the shortest ten hours and forty-four minutes. On the 12th of December the sun rises at 5° 22′ A. M. and sets at 6° 38′ P. M.: on the 12th of June he rises at 6° 38′ A. M. and sets at 5° 22′ P. M.: there is no twilight.

This beautiful island is one of the healthiest in the whole world, and if tropical diseases ever occur there, they rarely run their course with the violence that renders them so formidable in India.

It was early used as a Sanatarium for the unhealthy French settlements on the coast of Madagascar, and is still employed for the same purpose.

From its situation in the track of the trades it is liable to occasional hurricanes, lasting from twelve to fifteen hours with undiminished intensity, attended with great destruction to property. They are accompanied by torrents of rain, overflowing the rivers, which thunder down the ravines like cataracts, and for the time, intercept the communication between different parts of the island. The barometer is the surest indication of their approach, and the measure of their violence while they last, falling during the passage of an extraordinarily violent gust, and rising again immediately afterwards. Sugar houses, churches, and trees have been blown down by them, and ruin and devastation usually mark their track.

Each direction of the wind has its own meteorological character. The S. E. is almost always a dry, strong wind, rising at eight in the morning, and being replaced in the evening or night by the land breeze. During the steady continuance of a S. E. breeze, white stationary clouds are seen to the Eastward, covering the mountains with a dense veil, until they are dissipated by the land wind.

The N. E. is usually a rainy wind, blowing generally in January, February, and March, during the height of the rains. At this season of the year, it is accompanied by gentle showers.

The N. is also a rainy wind.

The N. W., W., and S. W. winds are usually rainy, especially during the hot season; they are hot, dry, unhealthy, and destructive to vegetation, burning the leaves of plants as if the blast of a furnace had passed over them.

From a table of the prevailing winds in 1818 and 1819, kept and constructed with much care, it appears that during that period, a North wind blew for 50 days, a N. E. wind for 170 days, an Easterly wind for 65 days, S. E. 275 days, S. W. 5 days, W. 13 days, N. W. 62; and there were calms for 89 days.

In the two succeeding years 1820 and 1821, the following is an abstract of the register of winds :— viz.

N.	2 days.	E. S. E.	148 days.	S. W.	1 days.	Variable, ..	89 days.
N. N. E.....	2 ,,	S. E.	262 ,,	W. S. W. ..	1 ,,	Calm, ...	8 ,,
N. E.	4 ,,	S. S. E.	76 ,,	W.	11 ,,		
E. N. E....	19 ,,	S.	1 ,,	W. S. W. ..	30 ,,		
E.	38 ,,	S. S. W....	2 ,,	N. W.......	2 ,,		

During the fine weather at Reunion, at sun-rise, the sky is clear, cloudless, and of the deepest azure tint; an easterly or south-easterly breeze springs up at 8 in the morning, light clouds gradually accumulate on the summit of the mountain of St. Denis, and ultimately spread like a thin veil nearly to the town; towards two in the afternoon it has every appearance of rain.

After sun-set the land breeze gets up, drives the clouds to the sea, and leaves the sky clear and resplendent with stars during the whole of the night. These phenomena are so regular in their occurrence, that there are scarcely ten fine days in any year, in which they are not witnessed in exactly the same sequence.

As most Englishmen are particularly interested in the state of the weather of every corner of the globe visited by them, the subjoined tabular statement will give invalids from India a tolerably fair average of the amount of sunshine and showers they may expect to find in Reunion.

Months.	DAYS.									
	Fine Weather.		Rain.		Cloudy.		Thunder.		Hurricanes.	
	1818	1819	1818	1819	1818	1819	1818	1819	1818	1819
January, ...	7	12	18	14	11	5	5	2	0	1
February, ...	8	9	16	13	9	6	5	0	0	0
March, ...	6	11	15	16	9	4	3	0	1	1
April, ...	8	12	11	13	11	5	3	0	0	0
May, ...	17	9	7	11	7	11	0	0	0	0
June, ...	17	17	4	7	9	6	0	0	0	0
July, ...	11	12	5	3	15	16	0	0	0	0
August, ...	18	11	3	14	10	6	0	0	0	0
September, ...	13	16	4	5	13	9	0	0	0	0
October, ...	22	14	5	2	4	15	0	0	0	0
November, ...	12	4	4	6	14	20	0	0	0	0
December, ...	11	12	13	12	7	7	0	1	0	0
Total, ...	150	139	105	116	119	110	16	3	1	2

The succeeding table gives sufficiently minutely the quantity of rain that fell during the years under review. Two-thirds of fine days in the whole year is so much more than the Englishman's average, that little fault will be found with Reunion on the score of rain. Eighteen inches is the largest quantity that fell in any single month.

Months.	Quantity of rain fallen.		Evaporation in the shade.		Number of days of rain.	
	1818	1819	1818	1819	1818	1819
	Inches.	Inches.	Inches.	Inches.		
January, ...	8.886	7.574	4.268	5.912	18	14
February, ...	6.402	4.197	3 561	5.723	16	13
March, ...	18.865	3.610	3.904	5.271	15	16
April, ...	4.383	3.437	3.437	3.774	11	13
May, ...	0.324	2.007	4.503	3.744	7	11
June, ...	0.559	2.925	4.436	3 344	4	7
July, ...	0.191	0.959	5.193	4.494	5	3
August, ...	0.124	1.772	7.018	4.598	3	14
September, ...	1.332	0.294	5.196	5.400	4	5
October, ...	0.533	0.107	7.887	6.859	5	2
November, ...	0.591	0.866	7.372	7.099	4	6
December, ...	8.326	7.709	6.212	4.834	13	12
Total,...........	50.516	35.457	62.987	61.052	105	116

The average temperature of the island is very uniform, the variations from month to month being comparatively trifling. This uniformity of temperature is among the causes of the great healthiness of Reunion, as there are few more efficient and formidable causes of certain classes of diseases, than sudden and extreme variations of heat and cold.

The following tables* give a fair estimate of the average and extreme variations of temperature during the several months of the years noted.

Mean indications of the Thermometer (Fahrenheit.)

Months.	Mean Minimum.		Mean Maximum.		Mean Temperature.	
	1818	1819	1818	1819	1818	1819
	o	o	o	o	o	o
January, ...	75.11	75.20	83.55	84.99	79.32	80.10
February, ...	76.30	75.15	85.62	85.82	80.96	80.49
March, ...	75.61	75.33	83.19	86.23	79.41	80.78
April, ...	73.71	72.10	83.77	82.81	78.74	77.45
May, ...	70.75	69.93	82.06	81.55	76.41	75.74
June, ...	68.86	67.39	79.34	79.29	74.10	73.33
July, ...	64.80	66.00	77.31	79.03	71.06	72.52
August, ...	66.16	66.13	79.30	78.71	72.73	72.42
September, ...	68.41	68.16	81.91	82.04	75.16	75.10
October, ...	70.97	69.89	83.19	83.48	77.08	76.68
November, ...	73.90	71.31	84.99	83.95	79.45	77.63
December, ...	75.70	73.58	85.26	83.86	80.47	78.72
Mean, ...	71.69	70.85	82.46	82.65	77.07	76.75

* This temperature is for the level of St. Denis : the observations were made in a covered, but otherwise exposed Verandah; the temperature of the hills is considerably lower, yet maintains the same uniformity.

Extreme variations of the Thermometer (Fahrenheit.)

Months.	1818 Maximum.	1818 Minimum.	1819 Maximum.	1819 Minimum.	Difference. 1818	Difference. 1819
	o	o	o	o	o	o
January, ...	87.71	71.96	88.70	71.78	15.75	16.92
February, ...	88.70	70 88	87.89	72.95	17.82	14.94
March, ...	87.98	70.25	90.68	70.52	17.73	20.16
April, ...	86.00	69.35	85.10	68.00	16.65	17.10
May, ...	83.03	67.28	86.54	65.03	15.75	21.51
June, ...	82.58	64.40	82.04	62.60	18.18	19.44
July, ...	79 25	61.34	81.86	61.88	17.91	19.98
August, ...	82.69	60.89	85.10	60.80	21.78	24.30
September, ...	85.73	64.49	84.92	64.40	21.24	20.52
October, ...	85.19	66.47	86.00	67.64	18.72	18.36
November, ...	87.35	69.80	86.72	67.10	17.55	19.62
December, ...	87.80	72.50	86.90	69.80	15.30	17.10

Although the progress of physical science has not yet succeeded in unravelling the mysterious connection between the magnetic phenomena of the earth, and the health or sickness of its inhabitants, barometrical measurements and oscillations are of considerable interest in reference to climate and meteorology. The following table,* which like all the above, is taken from the work of M. Thomas, is evidently the result of careful observation and record.

Extreme oscillations of the Barometer.

Months.	1818 Maximum.	1818 Minimum.	1818 Difference.	1819 Maximum.	1819 Minimum.	1819 Difference.
	Inches.	Inches.		Inches.	Inches.	
January, ...	29.898	29.655	.243	29 904	29.275	.629
February, ...	.866	.474	.392	.913	.643	.270
March, ...	30.064	28.734	1.330	.907	.405	.502
April, ...	29.946	29.717	.229	.980	.667	.313
May, ...	30.015	.682	.333	30.022	.757	.265
June, ...	.149	.831	.318	31.032	30.098	.934
July, ...	.213	.831	.382	30.158	29.884	.274
August, ...	.194	.882	.312	.200	.804	.396
September, ...	.162	.881	.281	.095	.844	.251
October, ...	.053	.788	.265	.130	.735	.395
November, ...	29.965	.729	.236	.038	.775	.263
December, ...	.940	.714	.226	29.971	.663	.308

* For the reduction of these tables to English standards, I am indebted to the kindness of Capt. Thuillier and Mr. V. L. Rees.

Mean indications of the Barometer.

Months.	At 6 A. M.		At 9½ A. M.		At 3½ P. M.		Daily mean oscillations.	
	1818	1819	1818	1819	1818	1819	1818	1819
	Inches	Inches.	Inches.	Inches.	Inches.	Inches.		
January, ...	29.820	29.746	29.828	29.778	29.775	29.723	5.35	5.51
February, ...	.735	.816	.764	.849	.698	.787	6.57	6.14
March, ...	.733	.803	.770	.836	.686	.769	8.27	6.77
April, ...	.865	.830	.886	.844	.812	.807	7.32	6.10
May, ...	.900	.864	.961	.906	.921	.837	7.48	6.89
June, ...	30.010	.968	30.051	30.011	.981	.947	6 97	6.46
July, ...	.059	30 015	.077	.064	.999	.987	7.91	7.71
August, ...	.047	.001	.069	.036	30.000	.961	6.85	7.52
September, ...	29.982	29.983	29.994	.019	29.924	.941	7.01	7.84
October, ...	.963	.932	.959	29.959	.903	.884	5.67	7.44
November, ...	.877	.924	.877	.947	.806	.881	7.17	6.61
December, ...	.826	.831	.839	.837	30.180	.765	5.28	7.20
Mean,..........	29.901	29.898	29.931	29.924	29.807	29.857	6.82	6.85

The population of the island of Bourbon, like that of other inter-tropical colonies, consists of whites, blacks, and mulattoes or half-castes. In 1826, the white colonists (French) numbered about 18,125 ; this portion of the population increases very rapidly, both by the arrival of new colonists from France, averaging fifty annually, and by the constant excess of births over deaths, the former being in the proportion of one to twenty-four of the whole white population, while the deaths amount to nearly one in forty-four and eight-tenths: the births being as to the deaths in the proportion of 179 to 100, or about 9 to 5. Upon an annual increase of 636 births, there were generally 83 natural children, or about one in every seven and two-thirds.

The 553 legitimate births are the fruits of about 154 marriages, which gives nearly one marriage to every 100 individuals, and an average of three children and six-tenths to each marriage. It is popularly believed that more girls than boys are born in hot climates ; this opinion is not borne out by the statistics of the island of Bourbon, since in a period of six years, from 1819 to 1824, a sixtieth more of boys than of girls were born there.

In 1824 the slave population of Bourbon was 45,375, it having decreased one-sixth in number from 1818, when it amounted to 54,359, and it was continuing to diminish at a still more rapid rate.

As the slaves were the only cultivators of the soil, this diminution was regarded with apprehension as likely very seriously to affect the extent of cultivation in the island and even to extinguish the rearing of produce requiring much labor and skill.

Two causes for the decrement were assigned—the small number of women, —the male exceeding the female sex in the proportion of 28 to 17 ; and the unsuitableness of the climate for the African population. The gross immorality of all slave states is not mentioned by the French writers, but doubtless was one of the most efficient causes of the mortality and diminution referred to.

A curious circumstance mentioned in the introduction to the work of M. Thomas is, that upon the capture of the island by the English in 1810, the number of freed-men was 2,340, whereas when the colony was restored to its former possessors in April, 1815, they had increased to 4,459. "So favorable," says the French Chronicler, "was the English rule to manumission: it has been otherwise since then, for during four years, from 1820 to 1823, twenty-three individuals only were liberated."

A recent paragraph in the Mauritius papers represents the immigrant population of Reunion to consist of—

	Indians.	*Africans.*
Men,..................................	17,827	998
Women, ...	1,529	181
Male Children, ...	168	19
Female Children, ...	119	17
	19,643	1,215

An impression appears to be entertained in India that the imported labouring population of Bourbon is reduced "almost to a state of slavery."

I believe this not only to be incorrect, but to be very unjust to the French Authorities. That they are compelled strictly to fulfil all obligations into which they enter, and are punished for every breach of contract is certain, but on the other hand they are protected from violence, injustice, or injury, and none of the punishments to which they are subjected are unnecessarily harsh or cruel. I was unable to collect any trustworthy information respecting the present number and condition of the free negro population. Those with whom I came in contact in the interior were a contented, idle, civil set, apparently as fond of finery and merriment as are the negro progeny in every quarter of the globe. *Maronage*, or the desertion of slaves has of course ceased, since all have been liberated, yet the old desire for a vagabond life seemed strong in many of those who have squatted in the ravines and almost inaccessible nooks that abound at every step. They are kindly treated by the Republican Government, and every effort is made to induce them to become industrious and peaceable subjects.

The earliest white inhabitants were convalescents from the French settlements in Madagascar, and the successful buccaneers of the 17th century, who carried the ill-gotten gains of their adventurous and criminal cruises to this retired island. They generally became quiet and peaceable settlers, who endeavoured to gain, by steady conduct and the externals at least of decorum and propriety, the good-will of the new community.

The agents sent out by the old French East India Company, many soldiers who became settlers, and the adventurers who usually flock to distant colonies as so many El Dorados in which rapid fortunes were supposed to be the certain result of migration, all aided to form the nucleus from which the present white Creole population is descended. The great healthiness of the climate is supposed to have induced many to become permanent residents who originally left Europe as birds of passage, with the intention of returning as soon as they had accumulated the means of living in comfort at home.

The descendants of the first Creoles are said to be an indolent race, with few wants, and those simple and easily satisfied. Their chief occupations are fishing, hunting, and the culture of rice and maize. As any species of work was, in their estimation, degrading to their character as whites, and as many of them in the days of slavery were unable to afford slaves, they retreated to the most retired places to conceal alike their poverty and their pride.

The possessions of their ancestors by constant division and subdivision became insufficient for the maintenance of their numerous families, or were sold to enable them more readily to divide the inheritance. They are described by M. Thomas, as well made, robust, and courageous; but full of pride, vanity, and touchiness. Their loyalty, filial attachment to the soil of France, capability of enduring fatigue and privation, and love of adventure, as seen in the exploits of the volunteer corps which distinguished itself in the old wars between France and England, are all lauded by the chroniclers of the island.

An amusing instance of the absurd pride of the class is current in the island. One of them, in a state of extreme indigence bordering on starvation, applied to a benevolent lady for charity. She gave him a bag of maize, upon which with the coolest impudence, he asked the loan of a slave to carry it for him. He was not ashamed to beg, but to bear a burthen in the presence of the slaves of the estate was an intolerable disgrace!

Formerly they were described as an extremely ignorant race, and good catholics without the slightest pretensions to any knowledge of the principles and precepts of religion. This is not the case at present; many of those with whom I conversed were intelligent, tolerably well informed, and in spite of the all-pervading vanity which peeps out on the smallest provocation, agreable and amiable.

As a race they seemed to me to be superior in energy, enterprize, and manliness to the corresponding class in India. Much of this is doubtless due to the superior salubrity of their climate. The enervating atmosphere of Bengal would dwarf a race of giants in three generations, if they lasted so long, and I believe there are not to be found in the plains of Hindostan, the descendants of pure European settlers, who can date their origin further back. The old attempts to encourage European invalids to settle and transmit a white population attached to and children of the soil, failed entirely.

On the other hand, the white Creoles of Reunion can, in many cases, trace back a direct lineal descent of undegenerated succession from the early settlers in 1717.

What an important lesson does this teach of the impolicy and folly of retaining and attempting to rear the healthy offspring of the European soldiery, in Calcutta, instead of producing a vigorous, manly population in the Hills, to form, hereafter, the nucleus of a great community of pure European descent. Such a barrier, existing between the dark races of the plains, and the hardy settlers of Central Asia, would in ages yet to come, exercise an important influence on the future destinies of the great Indian Empire.

It is remarkable that the same degeneration and decadence of the white race have been observed in Java, and in some of the West India Islands. In the former, the results of an extended and close official enquiry by the late Governor General of the Dutch possessions in India, elicited the fact, that the progeny in the third generation was almost entirely female, and that the majority of these were sickly and barren.

There seem to be few foreigners settled in Reunion. I only heard of four British residents in the island, and three of them, ladies, were Milesians. The fourth is a coachman who originally found his way to St. Denis in the capacity of a groom, in charge of horses from the Cape or Australia. This man is a perfect original in his way, and in the hands of Boz or Geoffroy Crayon would form an excellent type of a wandering Englishman isolated in a foreign land, amidst strange people, and entirely new associations. He is a first rate whip, well-versed in the mysteries of the road and ribbons, and in fact a sober sort of Sam Weller, with a touch of Mark Tapley in his composition.

He is not a little of a quaint humourist in his way, as we ascertained accidentally from his address to his team.

"Soho! Soho! gently Pascal! gently! why don't you behave like Newton, my beauty."

This strange association of names, upon enquiry, elicited the fact of his having thus christened his cattle.

The reason given for naming the wheeler after the gentle author of the Provincial Letters was singular enough. "He's a werry himpetuous hanimal, Sir, so I calls him Pascal to please the French, 'cos he goes like *Blazes!*"

Ye shades of all that is amiable and excellent! the most gentle and benign of philosophers, to become the godfather of a fiery steed.

The other Bucephalus was denominated from the proud manner in which he held his head and elevated his crest.

"He's a reglar star gazer, Sir, so I calls him Newton."

While descending one of the steep hills, Pascal became fidgetty and began to plunge. I could not see the cause, but was made acquainted with its nature by witnessing a most scientific flourish of the whip, followed by the humming of "FLY! not *yet*—'tis not the hour," which accompanied the removal of the source of irritation! Quite as quaint in its way as the quiet removal of the blue bottle that tickled the philosopher's nose, and was dismissed with the gentle injunction of the world being large enough for "thee and me!"

To return, however, to the physical characters of the island. Its surface is furrowed by many rivers and ravines, which radiating towards the sea, discharge themselves at various points in its circumference.

Between St. Denis and the burnt land on the weather side of the island there are no less than fifteen rivers, which, with the mists and showers abundant in their vicinity, render this quarter very productive and fertile.

Of the fifteen, but eight are large enough to deserve the name of rivers, less from the body of water they usually contain, than by reason of their length, the swiftness of their course, and their occasional rapid rise from temporary causes.

The river of the East, which is the limit betweeen the communes of Saint Rose and Saint Benoît, rises at the base of the plain of sands between the peak of the same name, the two small table-mountains, and the centre called Haüz: its length is about three leagues.

For some distance from its origin it is confined between the mountains, on emerging from which it flows to the sea on a broad bed in which it has excavated its channel in a tortuous course, winding right and left. So rapid are the changes in this course that a traveller, who, when crossing had the main stream before him, has seen it rush behind him so speedily as to have passed over dry shod. The river rises suddenly to a considerable height, and falls again almost as quickly to its natural level, its current is always rapid, and very dangerous to ford, as its bed is filled with large, loose, round stones.

The river of Marsoniers traverses the quarter of St. Benoît, rises in the centre of the island, and is from five to six leagues in length; it usually has little water in its channel, except in the rainy season when it becomes of respectable dimensions from the numerous streamlets pouring their contributions into its basin from the middle of the forests and the foot of the mountains.

Its banks are low, causing it occasionally to overflow and damage the neighbouring lands and dwellings. It is now crossed by a substantial bridge.

The river of Rocks has a more restricted course, and its banks are planted with trees from its source to its fall. Much rain falls in its immediate vicinity, from which its stream, always plentiful, is frequently raised, and its current rendered rapid and dangerous, large masses of loose rock being often carried along with it.

The river Dumas or du Mat, like the preceding, has its source surrounded by hills and forests: it has always a plentiful supply of water, its bed is large, its current rapid, and its fords were dangerous before it was bridged.

The river St. Jean which separates St. Andrè from Ste. Suzanne, runs quietly and in a somewhat muddy stream to the sea. In the rainy season its waters are greatly increased, and the more so as its gentle current causes the accumulation of the waters, faster than they are discharged. It is more easily forded than most of the other streams in the island.

The river Ste. Suzanne, after running for a considerable distance among the heights, at length, at about half a league from its embouchure falls in cascades upon the plain. After its descent it describes a very serpentine course to the sea. During the winter, this fall, which is more than a hundred and sixty feet in height, is said to have a very picturesque and romantic appearance.

The river of the Rains, which is generally invisible except from the dry ravines encumbered with rocks which intersect the road in its course, is sometimes a formidable stream. It arises between the plaine des Chicots and the plaine des Fougères, has a full stream in the mountains, and ultimately dips down into a vast bed of alluvium, whence its waters find their way subterraneously to the sea. When it rises from its deep recesses, which it does with loud and angry rumbling, it rapidly fills the various branches supplied by it, and runs with such impetuous impulse as to carry away every thing in its mad career, enormous rocks and the deepest rooted giants of the forest being hurled along helpless in its irresistible rush. It separates the communes of Ste. Marie and St. Denis.

The river of St. Denis is to the westward of the town, at the foot of the mountain which ends in forming Cape Bernard. It rises from the lower part of the plaine des Chicots, at a short distance from the source of the river des Galets. Like the river of the Rains it runs for some distance by itself between high hills. Usually a quiet stream, in the rains its bed is filled to such an extent as occasionally to interrupt the communication between the banks at its mouth. Its course, although serpentine, is there very rapid, and it soon empties itself.

There are various other streamlets in the part of country noticed, but they are too insignificant for special description, and undeserving of the name of rivers.

Of the five streams on the leeward side of the island, three are small and insignificant, and the remaining two only worthy of special mention.

The first, the river des Galets, rises in the mountains at a very short distance from the St. Denis stream, like which, it is long confined in its course. It falls into the plain at a noisy cascade, which, when the floods rise, roars incessantly. Its bed is then full, its waters raised, and its currents so rapid as to carry along rocks in its headlong career, and to become dangerous to cross.

The river St. Stephen, which separates the communes of St. Louis and St. Pierre, has its source at a great distance from its embouchure, beyond the mountains bordering the leeward side of Reunion. It runs between them for six leagues, and receives tiny tributaries which enlarge its stream to respectable dimensions near its mouth. Like the other rivers it rises in the floods, and then has an impetuous current. The mass of its waters are deflected, for purposes of irrigation, into a pretty and profitable canal, by which an arid and sterile region has been rendered fertile and productive.

Many of the streams mentioned above have alluvial beds formed by the detritus of the basaltic rocks and lava, partially decomposed. The rains causing the floods and torrents which break down and pulverize the rocks, wash away the soil from the mountains, and having reached the point of junction where the waters of the ocean arrest the progress of the rivers, deposit the fine soil previously held in suspension—hence the formation of patches of cultivable soil. The causes of their production have gradually diminished, and are not so frequent as they used to be formerly, particularly since the clearing of the forests has lessened the frequency and amount of the periodical rains.

It would be impossible to describe the innumerable ravines, many of which intersect the high road. The abundant rains formerly excavated those beds of the torrents, in which the water only lies during a few days in the winter season; for the rest of the year they are dry. Some are very deep, with scarped sides that render them difficult to scale from below. In most ramps have been raised to facilitate access to them.

The whole island, with the exception of a small inaccessible portion near the volcano is encircled by two great roads; the one near the sea-board, to facilitate the transport of produce to the ports and establish the defensive communications of the country; the other higher up, forming a second girdle, smaller and more tortuous than the first, with which it frequently communicates by paths and cross roads.

Many of the hills are scarped and roads formed along their sides, following in some degree the natural levels of the ravines. Some of them are on a grand scale, in excellent condition, and practicable for carts and carriages; others are mere foot and bridle paths, and from the natural difficulties of the ground can never be rendered more accessible than they are at present. The engineering difficulties on the windward side of the island were comparatively trifling, and there are consequently found the best and largest lines of communication. On the leeward aspect, the natural obstacles opposed so formidable a barrier to road-making that it was found impossible to do more than establish means of access for horsemen and pedestrians. The roads in general are in excellent preservation, constructed with much care and skill, and afford easy access to the different parts of the island.

Nearly the only exception is probably the most important of all—the Salazie road; and although even this presents no real difficulties of any kind,

a very little care and expense would render it more easy for invalids than it is at present. The bridges are numerous, in some cases solid, and in most instances safe and pretty structures, creditable alike to the skill and taste of the French engineers, and the wisdom of the authorities in overcoming natural obstacles to the freedom of inter-communication between the different parts of this difficult country. A few are of solid masonry capable

of resisting the perpetual floods of the rainy season; one or two are on the suspension principle; and many are wooden structures well suited for the different localities in which they occur.

The great want of the colony is a port, the only places of anchorage along the whole coast being open road-steads, all more or less exposed, and at certain seasons unsafe. The roads of St. Denis and St. Paul alone are frequented by large merchantmen, although there are several eligible anchorages for small vessels.

At St. Denis there are a couple of piers, and a small basin for boats, protected on the sea face by an enormously strong stone barrier, yet all this is insufficient to establish a constant communication with the shipping in rough weather. The eminent skill of the French engineers has failed to overcome the natural difficulties of the inaccessible coast, so that Reunioñ is destined to remain for ever, secondary in commercial and political importance to her neighbouring and beautiful sister.

Like the Mauritius, Reunioñ is dependent on other countries for the chief supplies of cattle and food. Madagascar contributes beef; the Cape, mutton, corn and horses; India, rice and gram; and France, wines and most of the minor necessaries and luxuries of life. The supply of grain and rice is sometimes at so low an ebb, as to lead to serious misgivings, and one of the first effects of a European war would most probably be to ruin and starve the colony. The impolicy of being so utterly dependent on esoteric resources for the means of physical existence, as are both islands, strikes every stranger, and renders it difficult to understand why some steps are not taken by their respective governments to remedy so perilous a state. Every thing is sacrificed to Sugar, and the time will most probably come when some terrible catastrophe will punish this unnatural craving for extracting the utmost gain the earth can be made to yield, for export.

Of the amount of the exports and imports of Reunioñ I know nothing, nor do I think they would be of much interest to the class of readers for whom this cursory sketch is intended, were I able to detail and translate them, as minutely as modern price currents and commercial registers accomplish for most British Colonies.

For the same reason I refrain from recording any of the circumstances connected with the agriculture of the island, and the interesting history of the various economical substances that have at different times formed the staple of its produce. In former times there were extensive and fertile pasturages in Bourbon, covered with flocks of sheep. Horned cattle were reared in considerable numbers, and the breeding of even horses was attempted. All this has now disappeared, and in the present depressed state of the colony, with the uncertain political condition of the mother-country, is not likely to be replaced.

Coffee, spices, and cotton, preceded the reign of sugar. The first of these is still cultivated to a small extent, and some of the samples which I saw and tasted were excellent in quality and flavour. The two latter have, I believe, almost entirely disappeared.

Rice and corn, once produced in tolerable quantity, have also been abandoned. Manioc, potatoes, maize and a few other products of the kitchen garden are still seen, and are all good of their kind.

Vanilla is only grown in small quantities, and fetches a high price. It is of superior quality, and large quantities would readily find purchasers in India. The island also produces excellent chocolate. Indigo was once attempted, but failed. Cinnamon also was formerly tried, and shared the same fate. The tea plant, introduced in 1819, throve well for some years in the botanical garden, but does not appear to have extended beyond it. This garden, as mentioned in a former page, is one of the most interesting and creditable establishments in the Colony.

In 1839 and the year following, a commission was sent by the government of Bourbon to Salazie, to select a suitable spot for a convalescent hospital. The chief of this expedition was a M. de Leissègues, the principal medical officer of the Colony at the time. I was unable when at St. Denis to obtain a copy of his report, but on my return was favoured with it by Mr. Piddington, after my own notes were prepared. It is so much more complete than the observations I was able to collect during my flying visit, that I have cancelled most of them, and will here present to my English readers the substance of M. Leissègues remarks, with a rambling commentary on some of his statements.

In general they coincide with my own views, and their accuracy is attested by the subsequent experience of the years that have elapsed, since the healing virtues of the waters were first established and made known.

That I have in no degree exaggerated the physical beauties of this happy valley, a fit abode for Hygeia, the goddess of Health herself, will appear from the following description of the French reporter:

"Salazie forms a great basin, about four leagues in diameter, circumscribed by the Salaze mountains. It is an extremely rugged, hilly, uneven country, by which although its surfaces are multiplied, its communications are rendered difficult. It has now, however, been so much cleared as considerably to have diminished its distance and difficulties. It is exceedingly woody, and watered by a multitude of fresh running streams, as well as some mineral springs, both hot and cold. The temperature of the valley is mild, resembling that of France in the month of May. It is a perfect paradise for the geologist, who would be transported with admiration in scaling its mountains, or scanning its ravines, genuine abysses, to penetrate into the very interior of the earth. The young botanist would experience the sweetest emotions in examining its endless variety of plants and flowers, with their elegant corollas, simple or multiple pistiles, and more or less numerous stamina, by their means identifying from among their sisters, those daughters of the woods who embellish with so much grace and beauty the great herbal of nature. Blind indeed must he be who, unmoved by the divine influences surrounding him, could attribute them to chance—chance which is nothing! No! No! At Salazie above all, the man of feeling is compelled to avow that every thing in the universe raises its voice to the Creator, and composes the hymn of gratitude sent up from earth to heaven! Of a surety, if bliss is to be enjoyed in this sublunary sphere it is at Salazie, a charming country, a new land of promise, where, were they so disposed, its happy denizens could soon send down to the neighbouring towns rivulets of milk and honey. To accomplish this they have only to prepare artificial meadows, or to sow good pasturages, an easy task where moisture is so abundant, and a perpetual spring, with its moderate heats, reigns supreme. By this means they could multiply flocks and herds; and cause gatherings of the busy bee sufficient to produce a large supply of the finest honey in the world, as experience has proved that they thrive well in this paradise.

"Nevertheless, the contemplation of the surrounding beauties with the exquisite sense of delight it calls into being, is alloyed by a feeling that something is wanting. The flowers, ravishing to the sight, are little scented, and there is no harmonious concert of birds, to break the sombre silence of the woods. The sage has said 'the eye is not satisfied with seeing, nor the ear filled with hearing.'"

The comparative absence of the feathered tribe is a remarkable feature of both islands, and in singular contrast with the teeming multitudes that enliven the woods of India. I do not remember to have seen even a crow or a sparrow, those inseparable companions of savage and civilized man in almost every accessible nook of the habitable globe. Sea birds abound, particularly in the islets adjoining the coast of Mauritius, and are chiefly of the gull tribe. Among them is the graceful paille en queue or boatswain bird, with its singular semblance of a marling spike for a tail. The common minas of Hindustan chatter and hunt in couples among the sugar canes, appearing quite at home with their sable companion, the Indian coolie. Green parroquets with a grey capuche, blackbirds which are made game of, and two or three varieties of pigeons, with a tame species of sparrow hawk, and the corbigeaux seem almost to complete the ornithological catalogue of these 'ocean gems.'

Mischievous monkeys people the ravines in the Mauritius, and the rats are as numerous and formidable as those who devoured the bold bad Baron famed in the legends of the Rhine :—but reptiles there are none.

The curse with which St. Patrick blessed the Emerald Isle extends to these happy regions, and to a sojourner from the Eastern abodes of snakes, centipedes, and all the creeping horrors of the tropics, it is an untold delight.

The fabled dodo was shrouded in mythical mystery, and I was not even favoured with a sight of the solitary bone by which its earthly career is proved.

The Madagascar bat, as large as an Indian flying fox, with its black sharp muzzle, large, bare ears, and hooked talon, is found in the Mauritius, and I believe also in Bourbon. Absurd tales of its vampire nature, blood-sucking qualities, and harpy-ish propensities are told and believed.

The coral reefs in the vicinity of the islands are singularly rich in marine products, and send excellent fish to the markets, but some of them are poisonous, and several not very palatable. The treasures of the deep have not yet by any means been ransacked or exhausted in this southern region, which still presents a fine field for icthyophagi and icthyologists.

In returning to Calcutta, on a fine, smooth, balmy day, we sailed over the great bank known to hydrographers as the 'Saya de Malha,' and I was astonished at the multitude and variety of fish, corals, madrepores and the innumerable inhabitants of the great ocean that literally swarmed in the nooks and recesses of the rocky bottom over which we glided. The brilliant transparency of the water revealed its tenants, tinged with every hue presented by the shining pearl and irridescent opal.

We did not find all the plants so devoid of odorous qualities as the French physician represents. The ferns, convolvuluses and similar 'sisters of the woods' were very much in this respect as they are elsewhere; but the air was perfumed with its most exquisitely scented zephyrs wherever

'beds of violets blue
And fresh blown roses wash'd with dew,'

diffused their fragrant charms, and exhaled their aromatic breath. This was especially the case in the spots, neither few nor far between, where

> " The blue-eyed violet weeps upon some sloping bank
> While the young sun dries up her tears !"

The twining honey-suckle also lent its aid to the spicy gales of the 'fair dew-dabbling blushing morn' on which we descended from Salazie.

The absence of the voice of any warbler of the woods to break with lute-tongued melody, the silent solitude of the shady groves, or to form a fitting accompaniment for the tinkling murmuring of the babbling rills

> 'that shun the light
> Stealing soft music on the ear of night,'

was certainly painfully felt.

'The Salaziens,' says M. Leissègues, 'are robust, hard-working and hospitable.' Among their good traits are enumerated, the religious care with which their children are brought up, and their simple, pastoral habits. One of these 'shepherds of Israel,' 's'ést improvisé medicin' and became the means of saving many lives that would have perished but for his skill. The improvised doctor of the period of our visit was the Commissary of Police of the district, who is also proprietor of the pavillions at the springs. He has some simple, and by no means inefficacious methods of treating ordinary cases, in which his efforts are aided by the pure air and medicated waters of the sanatarium.

If medicine be really, as some have asserted, the art of amusing the patient, while nature cures the disease, the race of Valentine Greatrexes would flourish, unapproached and unapproachable, by the genuine disciples of Esculapius, in the Salazie valley.

All classes and races seem to acquire vigour and restoration in its genial influence. Here the Creoles lose their effeminate forms, the Europeans convalescing from dangerous diseases regain their roses and robustness, and even the Negroes acquire a vigour and activity unknown to them elsewhere.

The height of the barometer varies little during the twenty-four hours in the valley, but the thermometer has an extended range in the same period. The following average of observations, made at different hours of the day, is contained in M. Leissègues' paper :

5	o'clock	in the morning	45°	Fahrenheit
6	,,	,, ...	50	,,
7	,,	in the shade	53	,,
8	,,	,, ...	57	,,
9	,,	,, ...	61½	,,
10	,,	,, ...	66	,,
11	,,	,, ...	73	,,
noon	,,	,, ...	77	,,

1	,,	in the afternoon	79	,,
2	,,	,, ...	77	,,
3	,,	,, ...	74	,,
4	,,	,, ...	72	,,
5—¼	,,	,, ...	67	,,
5+¼	,,	,, ...	60	,,
6	,,	,, ...	57	,,
7	,,	,, ...	55	,,
8	,,	,, ...	52	,,
9	,,	,, ...	50	,,*

The most striking difference, however, is noted between the temperature in the sun and in the shade at the same hour—a difference amounting to as many as nearly 50 degrees of Fahrenheit.

The moment the sun dips behind the lofty hills surrounding the funnel-shaped portion of the valley at the source, there is an immediate and rapid diminution of heat; and the same, in a minor degree, is perceived at about a quarter past seven, a few moments after the rise of the south-west land breeze.

There is generally a haze hanging over the valley in the evening, sometimes amounting to very fine rain. It is not so dense as the white fleecy mists that pour down and shroud the Kandian valleys in an impenetrable veil in a few moments. Towards the lower part of the Salazie it falls in the form of very fine, rapidly soaking, yet scarcely perceptible rain, more like a heavy dew than the outpouring of the moisture of the clouds.

As we found on approaching the island, the crests of the highest mountains are scarcely ever visible after sunrise. They are best seen when first lit up by the rays of the great luminary as he rises to the horizon: during the day they are usually concealed in a cap of mist, caused by the rising of the vapours of the valley, as the upper strata of the air become rarified by the increasing heat.

The supply of the mineral water from the spring seems to be nearly inexhaustible; it was estimated when we were there, at about a thousand pints an hour, from the small openings through which it was conducted.

The following analysis of the waters was given to me by M. Marcadieu, a distinguished chemist residing at St. Denis. It corresponds exactly with that publishel in the official report, and appears to have been the mean of the several analyses performed by Messieurs Marcadieu, Le Pivain, and Toulorge.

The quantity examined was a French litre, rather more than an English pint.

* These numbers are not absolutely exact, but sufficiently so to note the extreme differences mentioned.

Carbonic Acid Gas,........................	1.250
Fixed matter, ...	1.350
	2.600
The fixed ingredients were :	
Carbonate of Soda,........................	0.500
Carbonate of Magnesia,....................	0.430
Carbonate of Lime,........................	0.180
Carbonate of Iron,........................	0.020
Chloride of Sodium, ...	0.007
Sulphate of Soda, ...	0.030
Silica, ...	0.160
Vegetable extraction matter, a trace, ...	
	1.327
Loss in analysis, ...	0.023
	1.350

It is evident from this examination, which I repeated and verified as far as my limited means permitted, that the carbonate of soda exists in solution as a bi-carbonate, and that all the other carbonates are held in solution by an excess of carbonic acid.

It has also been shewn by analysis that during the rainy season the temperature of the waters, and the proportion of solid ingredients contained in them, diminish proportionally from the infiltration and admixture of the rain water.

The deposit which is almost immediately precipitated upon the escape of the excess of carbonic acid, consists chiefly of carbonate of iron, with very small quantities of the carbonates of lime and magnesia, and a little silica.

The mean temperature of the Salazie waters ranges from 25° to 28° degrees of Centigrade, or from 77° to 82.4° of Fahrenheit.

The waters of Cilaos which are situated at a level of eight hundred feet higher than those of Salazie, are richer in the proportion contained in them of the same mineral ingredients, and are of higher temperature, being in the baths formed extemporaneously by excavating a suitable hollow in the surface of the ground, about 102° of Fahrenheit. This was found to be a constant result.

The Salazie waters are very nearly identical in composition with those of the celebrated springs of Vichy in France, which have been renowned for ages, and are much resorted to by dyspeptics and invalids generally from all parts of Europe.

The diseases for which the French reporters consider the Salazie waters to be curative and proper, are, chronic enlargements of the liver and spleen biliary concretions, various renal and vesical affections, particularly those dependent on derangement of digestion, nephritic colic, chlorosis, amenorrhœa, habitual vomiting, intermittent and remittent fevers,—especially those complicated with abdominal obstructions. They are also supposed to be efficacious in certain affections of the joints, in the stiffness and immobility resulting from long disuse of a limb, and in certain cases of partial palsy.

As I have no intention of writing a professional treatise, and moreover have nothing new to advance upon the subject of the use of mineral waters, or of the effects of climate in the removal of disease, I do not dilate upon any of the abovementioned topics in this place.

The greatest care and discrimination are necessary in the selection of sanitaria, and particularly in the cases which are sent to them for cure or amendment. In these important matters I strongly recommend every Indian invalid to be guided by the opinion of his professional advisers, and not to trust to his own judgment and fancies, which are most likely to mislead him.

The climate of Bourbon is admirably adapted for restoring the health of those who have suffered from the endemic and epidemic diseases of India. In addition to a sea voyage of moderate duration in the delightful track of the trade-winds, it presents a considerable variety of climate, from the level of St. Denis on the sea-coast, to Cilaos and Salazie in the mountains.

The fine season commences in May, or about the latter end of April, and outlasts the unhealthy and trying seasons in Bengal. The traveller from India leaving late in February or in March, would most probably avoid the chances of storms or hurricanes, and reach Bourbon at the beginning of the cool weather. The distances in the island are short, the places of resort for invalids easily accessible without much fatigue or exposure, the cost of living within the compass of most Indian officers, and in all respects it is a most desirable and eligible refuge. When to these advantages is added the inestimable value of its mineral waters for those cases in the cure and removal of which they are known to be efficacious, I am strongly persuaded that in many respects it will be found a more eligible resort, in a mere sanitary point of view, than even England itself.

The condition which is most likely to be benefited by the sea voyage, climate of Bourbon generally, and mineral springs of Salazie and Cilaos in particular, is the state of pallor, languor, and prostration of mind and body, that is the most frequent condition of Europeans who have resided long in India, or suffered from its severest maladies.

The sallow, exsanguine countenance; dull, pearly, lifeless eye; listlessness, torpor, despondency, irritability, and utter incapacity for the performance of official duties requiring mental energy and application, with the imperfection of digestion and its train of attendant ills, down to the occurrence of severe neuralgic pains in various parts of the body, found in these cases, are all removed, and the functions restored to a state of healthy, vigorous action, unknown to the 'lean and slippered pantaloon,' since he came out a fair, rosy, laughing cadet, or a roistering inmate of the College of Fort William.

It is still more directly and certainly favourable in the whole host of maladies to which ladies are liable, and which may properly be denominated 'female complaints.'

The life of inactivity, seclusion, and utter ennui to which most of the fair sex are doomed in India, rapidly converts their roses into lilies, and leaves them pale, and etiolated as a flower deprived of light.

It is scarcely possible to imagine any habits more certainly destructive of health than those of the wives and grown up daughters of European sojourners in this land of the sun. Those who rise early, and ride or walk before his scorching rays drive all who are not compelled to brave and 'mock his majesty,' to seek the protection of the shade, are comparatively few. The majority seldom stir abroad until the evening; pass the day in the most enervating, inactive occupations, and the whole exercise they take is the gentle movement of a carriage in the daily drive. The evening is devoted to a hot, heavy, unwholesome dinner, at which the guests are more likely to die of ennui than from repletion, and occasionally polkas and waltzes are performed with the thermometer at 90° F. under the punkah; the whole operation being not an unapt representation of a dance in a vapour bath.

And yet it is expected that such an utter disregard of the simplest dictates of nature, and violation of her most evident and intelligible operations should be consistent with a state of health.

In short, the ills which are susceptible of being permanently and radically cured by the course I recommend, are, all incipient diseases of a functional nature, the most common sequels of every variety of fever common to or occurring in India, where the important and vital organs of the body are not spoiled by irreparable changes in their structure; the ordinary results of cholera, liver disease, prolonged fluxes, rheumatic affections, and the state called 'cachexia' by the faculty. It does not appear to be so well adapted for confirmed pulmonary affections, and is necessarily of no use in malignant diseases, or in the wasting of advanced years.

THE MAURITIUS.

My original design has been accomplished, and I trust I have, in my rough and imperfect sketch of Bourbon, succeeded in convincing my Indian readers, that the greatest of all earthly blessings, health, is within the easy reach of those who have been so unfortunate as to part with it from the invasion of any of the plagues and pestilences of this land of malaria.

The sister-island of Mauritius is so well known, and has been so often described, that I should have hesitated to record my impressions of it, were it not that the approaching establishment of steam communication, uniting it with India on the one hand, and the Cape of Good Hope on the other, invests it with a peculiar interest at the present time.

When brought within a few days sail of Hindustan, this beautiful and prosperous possession will, I feel convinced, become the frequent resort of many who require a change of air and scene, and are unable to devote a large amount of time or money to the renewal of their faded energies and jaded spirits. It possesses many advantages over our hill sanitaria; is, in some respects, superior to the interior of Ceylon; is, in all points of view in advance of the Cape, in addition to being little more than half the distance; and for the same reasons is preferable to the Australian Colonies, although the latter, when bound to India by the steam chain that is now encircling the whole habitable globe, will probably be preferred by those whose tastes are of the pure Anglo-Saxon type.

After several days of anticipation and delay, following a hurried descent from Nuwera Ellia, on the 1st of March 1851, I descried in the distance a small schooner staggering along under a pigmy pyramid of canvas, attempting to make the harbour of Galle before sunset. As seen from the highest and most picturesque of the green hills in the neighbourhood of the commercial port of Ceylon, she seemed a tiny, rakish, 'skimmer of the seas,' such as Cooper delighted to paint, and buccaneers were wont to patronize. This was the mail schooner from Port Louis, the only direct means of communicating with the Mauritius during the hurricane season. Her burthen was little more than a hundred tons, and her short flush deck, high bulwarks, towering spars, and wild-looking crew, composed of representatives from half the maritime nations of Europe, with a sable cook of the most approved Æthiopian pattern, would have rendered one suspicious of her character on piratical cruising grounds.

She remained four days at Galle, wind bound, and at daylight of Wednesday the 5th of March, glided slowly and quietly out of the old Dutch port, under charge of a consequential dignified Pilot, of tawny complexion and pompous address.

The blue hills of Ceylon, picturesque and occasionally fantastical in form, faded from our sight in the course of a few hours, and I was once again, after an interval of ten years, sailing towards the Southern Hemisphere.

I had never before been cooped up in so small a craft, and soon discovered that those whose maritime experience is confined to floating castles, can form little idea of the grandeur and ceaseless roll of the great ocean. When there was barely a ripple on the face of the waters, and the heavy flapping of the sails fell dull and dreary on the ear, the schooner rolled on the long swell of the calm sea to an extent that often threatened to cast her tall masts into the dark abyss around her. With a moderate breeze on the quarter, she was steady and quiet, and cut her way through the blue sea with a pleasant, cheery sound, and a wake nearly as straight and foaming as that of a steamer.

But, at all other times, she pitched and tossed, and groaned, and creaked, like a troubled spirit, without a moment's rest. This I endured, under the burning sun of the equatorial latitudes, for the space of twenty-one days and nights.

To add to the delights of the passage, we had carried a full cargo of mosquitoes from Galle, who refused to be dislodged by all the smoking and other devices industriously applied to drive away those untiring plagues of humanity. The vessel leaked and was pumped out every two hours, day and night, until the clanking of the chains, the swash of the water upon the unsteady deck, and an occasional drenching as if from a water-spout, in the midst of a troubled dream, filled the mind with images of shipwreck, and peopled the dark, hot, ill-ventilated air of the cabin, with all the hideous monsters of the fabled caverns of the deep.

The prudent rats and sagacious cock-roaches had evidently landed in Ceylon, unwilling to trust themselves in so frail a tenement. The two monkeys pined and died; the fowls grew thin, melancholy, stony-eyed, and given to prolonged meditation on a single leg; the ducks declined to quack and consumed their own fat; and on the nineteenth day the last squeak of our solitary pig broke like an unearthly shriek on the still ear of the dark night, as if the disembodied spirit of an evil frame had quitted the abode of death.

The constant succession of squalls and calms, the loud roar of the fitful blast, when 'the sails did sigh like sedges,' and the drenching down-pour of the black clouds that deluged us as if with waters 'shot from some high crag,' would have cured the veriest Robinson Crusoe of all desire of a more intimate acquaintance with the mysteries of a sea-life, at the southern extremity of the zone of the periodic rains, during the hurricane months.

The only passengers, besides myself, were a young French Creole, given to gasconade and cock-fighting, and a grave, taciturn, middle-aged Arab merchant, a deck passenger, who bore up with the most exemplary patience against the discomforts of our chequered voyage. His whole worldly treasures were contained in a large teak wood chest which he never abandoned voluntarily for a moment. Many times and oft was he washed away by the heavy seas shipped over the bows, but in a moment he had scrambled back again, with his eyes intently fixed on the object of his solicitude, which was in truth the Mecca of his maritime existence.

On its lid he washed, dressed, eat, drank, prayed, and slept with unsurpassable devotion. His stock of provisions consisted of a bag of rice, and a large basket of dried cakes, with a small store of spices and condiments, all within arm's reach of his citadel. His plantains, pumplenoses, and cocoanuts were stowed away in one of the quarter boats, and soon devoured by the monkeys, the Creole boy, and a young sea-imp yclept Bob, as full of tricks as his quadrumanous companions. This constant larceny never for a moment drew Mustapha from his lair, to which he seemed magnetically fixed. The glare of his dark eyes, and the savage scowl upon his swarthy brow, as he watched the gradual disappearance of his delicacies, embodied all the evil passions of an Arab nature, but were like the angry menace of a distant storm. At times he looked the very incarnation of the ancient mariner himself. He came on board as sleek and portly as a proud, well-fed Janissary, but left us as thin, grizzled, and care-worn as a half-starved, hunted, sleepless Bedouin of the Desert.

At length, on the 26th of March, when within three hundred miles of our destination, we found ourselves on the outer edge of a Cyclone. The uncontrollable gusts of the roaring wind, the dark, inky, murky, leaden loom of the distant horizon to windward, the magnitude of the rolling waves that at one moment raised us to the brink of a frowning precipice, and the next hurled us into the dark abyss of an overshadowed valley, where all was still and gloomy, and the angry strife of the elements shut out in an instant were sublime and grand to witness. I had been in storms before, but had never witnessed such a sea as this. It was a sight worth seeing, and can never fade from my memory, as I recall the deep and intense interest with which its awful features were stamped upon my mind. It fully realized the splendid passage in the Ancient Mariner :

> " And now the storm-blast came, and he
> Was tyrannous and strong :
> He struck with his o'ertaking winds,
> And chased us South along."
>
> " With sloping masts, and dipping prow,
> As who pursued with yell and blow
> Still treads the shadow of his foe,
> And forward bends his head,
> The ship drove fast, loud roar'd the blast
> And Southward aye we fled."

On, on we sped until at noon a faint, bluish, dwarfed mound was seen on the horizon, the first welcome sight of land. It gradually became more distinct, until about four in the afternoon we passed within half a mile of Serpent island, so called because a snake has never been seen upon it, and another small, barren rock shaped like the carapax of a tortoise, perfectly bare, and covered with sea birds, who shrieked, and sailed, and skimmed around us in all their graceful movements. The large waves breaking in spotless foam over the scarcely sunken reef, or thundering up the steep side of the abrupt rock, and falling back in a vast cascade of spray reflecting the rainbow tints of the setting sun, were singularly beautiful, after the wide waste of heaving waters on which the eye had rested, with wearied gaze, for so many days.

Shortly after dusk, we sailed through the shadow of the frowning bluff of the Gunner's Coign, and suddenly found ourselves gliding along in smooth water under the lee of the mainland. The change was almost painful, and, as we gently stole along the coast, inhaling the balmy breath of the earth, sheltered from the boisterous influence of the open ocean, thoughts of home, and peace, and many past scenes, imperceptibly stole over me, and kept me musing on the deck the whole of the night.

At day-break we were off the harbour of Port Louis, with all our signals flying, and as soon as it was sufficiently light stood in to the bell buoy marking the entrance through which alone the reef-girt port can be approached. A steamer soon put off to tow us in, and a pilot compelled us to hoist a yellow flag, in proof of our bill of health being unsatisfactory. A couple of cases of small-pox had occurred in the gravets of Galle, and this was sufficient to render us objects of suspicion. I soon explained the matter to the Port Surgeon, a sensible, well-informed member of my own profession, and he at once allowed us '*pratique*,' or communication with the shore.

I have once before remarked upon the monstrous absurdity with which the quarantine laws are enforced in the Mauritius, and the ridiculous dread with which the Creoles regard the approach of contagious disease. In so limited a community small-pox ought to be eradicated, or rendered as harmless as it is in the magnificent island of Java, where the energy and wisdom of the late Dutch Governor caused the vaccination of the entire population, whence all fear of this great curse has ceased.

The only sensible and efficient preventives against cholera, and the contagious fevers, few in number and diminished in influence in tropical latitudes, are drainage, ventilation, and cleanliness. The two latter are grievously neglected in the habitations and persons of the labouring classes throughout the island: the first has not met with the attention it deserves and requires.

The domestic arrangements of most houses, from the highest to the lowest, in Port Louis, in some essential particulars not necessary to detail here, are disgusting, and such as cannot fail, upon the supervention of any future epidemic, to decimate the population. Unless the Health Committee, appointed since I left the island, look well to these matters, I am convinced, from long familiarity with the causes and consequences of disease, that the pent up plague will be generated within the barriers of the foolish quarantine, and the citadel surrender without a struggle, surprized by an enemy rising in the very centre of its own strong-hold.

In no place that I have ever visited can all the essentials of the highest state of health be so surely and certainly commanded, from an unlimited supply of water, with fall enough to sweep away every thing before its cleansing and purifying influence, to the clear, bright, untainted air of heaven, as transparent as it is wholesome and invigorating to breathe.

Of the moral effects of sanitary legislation, it has been truly and elegantly said in contrasting the social influence of preventive and precautionary measures, with the ancient attempts to flee from pestilence, or to impede its progress by isolation, that "the former brings out all the kindly, generous, sympathetic elements of the human heart—the latter all that is selfish, hard, remorseless," and it might with equal point have been added, 'unsound, unphilosophical, and absurd.'

The admirable paper of Dr. Bowring read before the British Association in 1838, contains remarks applicable to quarantine regulations and the useless misery they inflict upon all their unhappy victims, in every part of the world. The result of considerable experience regarding their utter inutility, induced him to record the following sentiments, which I strongly recommend to the earnest consideration of the contagionists of 'la belle Maurice.'

"The pecuniary cost," he says, "may be estimated by millions of pounds sterling in delays, demurrage, loss of interest, deterioration of merchandize, increased expenses, fluctuation of markets, and other calamitous elements;

but the sacrifice of happiness, the weariness, the wasted time, the annoyance, the sufferings inflicted by quarantine legislation—these admit of no calculation—they exceed all measure. Nothing but their being a security against danger the most alarming, nothing but their being undoubted protection for the public health, could warrant their infliction; and the result of my experience is not only that they are useless for the ends they profess to accomplish, but that they are absolutely pernicious; that they increase the evils against which they are designed to guard, and add to the miseries which it is their avowed object to modify or to overcome."

This is now the well-established view of every man of eminence and ability, capable of forming or entitled to express an opinion on the subject.

The great main drains of Port Louis, bordering on the Company's garden, running behind the barracks, and permeating the purlieus of all that part of the town, are a source of far greater mortality and permanent mischief, than would result from the arrival of a whole fleet of coolie ships laden with cholera and small-pox, for these are the only diseases susceptible of propagation, which they are capable of carrying.

While I was at Port Louis a low type of typhoid fever was raging, which carried off a large number of the poorer classes. It had received at Port Louis and at St. Denis a variety of absurd names, all indicative of a blind desire to attribute it to a foreign source, instead of looking nearer home for the real solution of the mystery. It was denominated the Bombay fever, the Chinese fever, and several similar soubriquets referring to its supposed origin. It ought to have been called the fever of the filthy habits, unventilated cabins, and ill-drained localities of the lower orders of the town; for whatever may have been its immediate exciting cause, it would have passed harmless over the place, if the proclivity to such diseases had not existed, ready formed, to welcome its arrival.

I heard an amiable old French lady, herself a valetudinarian, attribute all the diseases of the island to the advent of Indian coolies, and she expressed a belief that some devastating epidemic was at hand, so much had the public health deteriorated from the good old times, when every one died of sheer antiquity, and the Mauritius was the abode of happiness, slavery, and health. This seemed a pretty general opinion among the Creoles with whom I conversed.

The remedy is in their own hands. Cleanse, ventilate, drain, and close the grog shops, and the island may safely defy the whole of Pandora's box of human miseries, as well as throw open her ports at all times and at all seasons to the stranger, without let, hindrance, or enquiry.

The first view of Port Louis, with the quaint circle of grotesque hills under which it is concealed, is singularly pleasing and pretty, and impressed me with a sense of the beauty of this charming island, that improved and was strengthened by a longer acquaintance with its varied features of excellence.

To describe it is not an easy task. The first illustration of this brochure conveys a tolerably correct idea of its aspect from the inner harbour, but is on too small a scale to convey any real estimate of the picturesque panorama that greets the eye in every direction.

We anchored close to the Custom House, were conveyed to the shore in an orthodox boat, and followed our baggage, carried by half-naked negroes, to the Hotel d'Europe, traversing the Place d'Armes, passing by the Government House and Post Office, and reaching our destination a little beyond the Theatre, next door to the Great Jail.

The hotel is tolerably large, and has one or two fine public rooms, but the sleeping apartments are small, ill-ventilated, and very close, with, in some of the ranges, thin panel partitions.

I had scarcely set foot on shore when I found out that I was in one of the most extravagant places in the world, where the practice of skinning a stranger is performed to perfection, and the most preposterous value is attached to the simplest offices, with a refreshing amount effrontery. My first day's experience was purchased at a ruinous rate for a subaltern's pocket. The transport of myself and baggage to the hotel cost me ten shillings—a drive of an hour and a half, in a hackney carriage, nine shillings; 'mundifying my muzzle' by the politest of Figaro's, two shillings, and cutting my hair, the same amount. The black cook on board the schooner, a finished *artiste* in his way, would have done the whole quite as well for six pence.

The shops are good and well supplied; the arrangements are entirely on the European plan, but the price of almost every thing is ridiculously extravagant.

Port Louis, or Saint Louis as the town is called, is situated on the north-west side of the island, and occupies the greater part of an extensive valley surrounded by lofty basaltic hills, the chief of which are the Pouce and Pieter Botte. These mountains are at present for the most part perfectly bare, and, with the exception of the head of Pieter, easily accessible. From the summit of the Pouce a magnificent view of the different districts of both the lee and weather sides of the island, as well as of the town and forts is obtained, with a boundless expanse of blue sea surrounding it. The extreme transparency of the atmosphere renders the sight one of the most charming and picturesque that can possibly be imagined.

The quays on which the stranger lands, are extensive, and well adapted for the traffic of this busy port. On the left hand are the custom house, marine offices, and large sheds for the sale of merchandize;—to the right are merchants' offices, and in front is the pretty place d'armes, planted with trees on either side, with a broad carriage way running between grass plats. The whole is terminated by the Government House, flanked by the public offices. The main guard, public library, commercial rooms, commissariat offices, and mercantile houses occupy the sides of the

Place. At its end and near the vice-regal residence is a stand of hackney carriages, well appointed and in some cases even elegant, but with too great a penchant for ultra marine and vivid colors. They are of great convenience to a community possessing comparatively few private equipages, but the charge of hire is so unnecessarily high as to limit their use.

The Government House is one of the most unsightly, inelegant structures in the place. It forms three sides of a square in front, enclosing a paved

courtyard, lined with verandahs on each floor. It has a pent roof, and although some of the rooms are large and well furnished, it is upon the whole little better than a three-storied barn. In the left hand corner of a small garden in front is a flag-staff, to notify by the hoisting of the national colours the presence of the Queen's representative, or to indicate his absence by the disappearance of the flag. The staff of His Excellency consists of a private secretary and one aide-de-camp :—there is little of pomp or parade attached to the office of ruler of the colony.

The government offices are located in mean, shabby-looking out-houses, less commodious and cheerful in their interior, than the opium godowns of Calcutta, or those of many merchants in this city. The post-office is a small, but much neater structure, placed near the port, adjoining the treasury, and apparently well adapted for its purpose.

The best thing in the town for its peculiar object is the market-place, which is divided into separate compartments and surrounded by a light iron railing. It is clean, well supplied with water, and forms altogether a most creditable institution. It would be difficult to imagine a greater contrast than exists between it, and the dirty, crowded, ill-ventilated bazaars of the so-called city of palaces.

The fountains in the town are constantly playing, and are cool, refreshing, and apparently well supplied with clean, pure, sparkling water. At the head of the basin bordered by a portion of the quay is one for the supply of water to the shipping; it is well constructed, easy of access, and seems inexhaustible.

The streets are straight, and run for the most part at right angles, the generality of them have commodious footpaths with a raised curb-stone to protect the passengers from the drains and the carriages in the road way. In some of the streets the houses have small, but neat and pretty court-yards in front, in most instances planted with trees and flowering shrubs, many of them from India. They give a picturesque and rus-in-urbe character to the town.

The interior of the houses is very much the same in character as that of residences of a similar class in St. Denis, but the rooms are larger, and there is a greater display of luxury and wealth in furniture and ornaments. In India they would be considered small, close, and confined, as they are indeed there in the hot season; but for the greater part of the year, they are well adapted to the climate, and sufficiently great for all real purposes of utility. Almost all the recent buildings are of stone, and some seemed to be not without pretensions to architectural taste, and even elegance of design. The Champ de Mars at the upper end of the town is bordered by houses, situated in luxuriant gardens, indicative of the comfort and wealth of their occupants. The Major General commanding the forces lives in the best of them.

The native part of the town has a singular appearance on entering the port, when the detached cabins are seen looking in the distance being like ill-shaped children's toys. They run for some little distance up the side of the hill, are built of wood, and are not very much in advance of the mud huts of tropical countries.

The floors of the houses of the higher classes are usually of wood, waxed and polished as in Paris. The ground floor of the hotels is laid with marble, and the walls are ornamented with gaudy coloured landscapes, battle pieces, and similar devices on coarse paper. In the better order of private houses, the papering is chaste, tasteful, and of every possible variety of pattern. The naked white-washed walls, and unsightly beams and burgers of Indian houses are not seen.

The members and higher functionaries of the Government, as well as most of the merchants, live in the country, driving in to their offices every morning. Some of the rural residences which I visited in the Plains Wilhelms and Moka districts were perfect types of all that is desirable and to be envied by those condemned to the unsightly bungalows and comfortless dwellings of Mofussil stations in Bengal and the Upper Provinces. They are beautifully situated, in elegant, ornamental gardens, command enchanting prospects, and contain all that can minister to the creature comforts. Banishment and exile cease to deserve their names when applied to the life in the Mauritius, of those whose means are adequate to enable them to live in such abodes.

The ordinary arrangement of the houses consisted of a drawing room, dining room, and the sleeping apartments varied according to the size of the dwelling—with a detached pavilion for visitors, containing one or more bedrooms. Some are snug little cottages, others on a large scale and furnished with every comfort, and even luxury that can render them desirable.

The churches of Port Louis are plain, unpretending structures, more useful than ornamental. Some of the little chapels dotted about the island are without the smallest pretensions to any thing like an approach to beauty of design, and in some instances are quaint, and even positively ugly. The most thorough going disciples of John Knox and the ancient Cameronians could not more effectually have banished all pertaining to ornament, or calculated to captivate the senses, than have the architects of the chapels at Moka and Plains Wilhelms.

The former is placed in a commanding position, is conspicuous from afar, and an eye-sore to the charming prospect around it. The exterior, however, is of little real importance compared with the influence upon the community of religion and her ministers, and in this respect, I am bound to say, that the Mauritius deserves a much higher degree of credit than is usually allotted to her.

The French retain their peculiar habits and sentiments in all parts of the world; but it is quite a mistake to imagine Port Louis the modern Capua it was represented to be in former years. Slavery and vice have always co-existed: liberty has produced her chastening influence where once she was unknown, and I believe the result to have been one of unmixed good in improving the morals, and correcting the manners of the colony.

There, as elsewhere in the present day, the clergy of the church of Rome have been most active in extending and consolidating the influence of their faith. Their success appears to have been great, particularly with the fair portion of the community, for the fasts and abstinence from worldly amusements during the season of Lent were so rigidly observed, that during the greater portion of my stay, Port Louis was as solemn and serious as a beleaguered city, clothed in sackcloth and ashes. On three several occasions in a tolerably well filled theatre, I could not count more than half a dozen ladies, and there was not a single ball, concert, or other species of pastime to break the dull monotony of existence. The season of gaiety certainly had not arrived, yet there was an unnaturally sober Saxon seriousness about the place, altogether antagonistic to the lively, mercurial, laughter-loving propensities of the Creole race.

The Queen's birth-day ball given at the Vice-regal palace is the signal of the breaking up of the ice of reserve and restraint, and when once set in movement, the current of gaiety is said to be rapid and incessant. As in Reunion the Creoles are passionately addicted to dancing and display, and most of the Pauls and Virginias of the island are reported to pinch and starve themselves for nine months, to launch out during the remainder of the year in all the glory of the brightest prismatic tints, for the most gorgeous and glaring colours seemed to be preferred to the sadder and more subdued hues of the chromatic scale.

The coolies keep up few of their own festivals and indeed lose much of the characteristics of caste which they carry with them. They have one grand scene of riot and revelry called Yamsey, which occurs once a year and lasts for eleven days. From the description I heard of it, I conjectured it to be a mixture of the Mohurrum and Ram Lela, with all the accompaniments of a great Indian fair.

The fete de Dieu and races I did not see. The latter have considerably diminished in interest and importance since the great commercial crisis ruined the principal merchants and landed proprietors of the colony. The race course and review ground are on the Champ de Mars, a bare space at the upper end of the town immediately below the base of the hills, to the sides of which it gradually slopes. It is a charming spot, the fashionable promenade of the present generation, and was the duelling ground of the old race of buccaneers and ruffians of which the island was once the stronghold.

The Theatre is a neat, commodious building, capable of holding a tolerably large audience. There was a very fair provincial company acting during the time of my visit, but they were not much patronized by the community at large. The theatre has usually been the arena where the Gallic and Antigallic feelings of the French and English sections of the community, have found vent. Several such demonstrations are recorded, and exhibit a sad want of sense and dignity on the part of the performers. One scene occurred shortly before my arrival, in which the absurd gasconading and pretensions of young Mauritius were well shewn. There is a general propensity all over the world on the part of the rising generation to assume a distinct individuality, which may fairly be classed among the popular delusions of the age we live in. It has penetrated to this little Peddlington of the Indian ocean, in the form of a bad imitation of Young England and the 'gamin de Paris.' The questionable interference of military authority gave an eclat to the matter, of which it was quite undeserving. The Saxon method of dealing with bravado and bluster would soon have put a stop to all such unseemly and offensive displays of nationality; and the good sense and good feeling of a community now bound together by many ties of union and interest, should set the seal of disapproval upon all departure from the strict path of courtesy and mutual consideration.

Deer hunting and coursing, both on foot, are among the field sports still indulged in, but neither are very exciting or entitled to be classed with the 'venery' of India. The absence of game renders shooting also a tame and spiritless pastime.

Port Louis possesses two reading rooms and libraries, which are accessible to strangers on liberal terms. The chief library is well stocked with an interesting collection of French and English works, is much frequented by the residents of the place, and is a well managed institution.

There are likewise two excellent museums in the town; one of natural history in the college, the other the property of M. Liénard, the elder. The former is under the charge of Mons. Bojer, the well known botanist, and is worthy of his great and widely established reputation. It is particularly rich in the corals, mandrepores, and marine productions of the neighbouring reefs, and contains some rare specimens of zoology from Madagascar, the Lemurs of which are celebrated for their beautiful furs and interesting zoological relations. Mons. Liénard's is more heterogeneous in character, and is a monument of his taste, liberality and enthusiasm in scientific pursuits. It contains an extensive collection of fishes, a few good pictures and articles of virtû, with numberless curiosities, sufficient to stock the cabinet of half a dozen astrologers of old. He is himself the beau ideal and type of a race now nearly as extinct as the Dodo itself. He has recently devoted himself with all the ardour of an enthusiastic nature to the investigation of mesmeric phenomena, and has accumulated a large number of observations on the subject. Some of those which he mentioned to me were sufficiently startling, although not such as to convince me that his investigations were free from numerous and serious sources of fallacy. His own entire good faith and scrupulous accuracy, it were impossible to doubt. I assisted at a magnetic séance in his house, when a middle-aged Creole female in a state of clairvoyance prescribed for various sick people who were not present, and gave a graphic diagnosis of their complaints, to the friends who came to apply for her counsel. The whole proceeding was singular and impressive. The clairvoyante was seated in a chair, under the influence of the magnetizer, and professed to be unconscious of the presence of those around. At a small table on her right hand side sat a secretary to note and record all that occurred. The friends of the sick were introduced silently, and seated on her left hand. I was so placed as to be able to observe all that passed, without taking part in the proceedings. The manipulations for entrancing the clairvoyante were similar to those frequently exhibited in Calcutta and elsewhere. When she was brought into the divining state, the applicants began by stating their names and places of residence, upon which the clairvoyante was directed to transport herself to the spot referred to, and to mention all she saw, which she did, in most instances with perfect accuracy. She then described the patient, indicated the disease, detailed the treatment and regimen to be observed, and answered through M. Liénard, who alone was in rapport with her, any questions that were asked of her. When each case was completed, the applicant deposited a small fee upon a stool near the clairvoyante, and departed in the most entire faith and reliance.

In one or two instances the sex and age of the distant patient were mistaken, and in the only extraneous test to which she was subjected, namely to transport herself to Calcutta, and give me a description of a person and place with whom I was acquainted, she was wrong. The whole proceeding would not bear analysis or investigation, and the accumulation of a century of observations so conducted, will never advance nor establish the truth of the doctrines of Mesmer. Mons. Liénard's object is a most praiseworthy one, and the good purpose to which he devotes it cannot fail to produce respect, even where it does not succeed in carrying conviction.

In addition to the museums above-mentioned, there are two or three rich and beautiful collections of land and water shells in the possession of gentlemen in the island.

The community is certainly intellectually inclined, and various societies exist for the cultivation of art and science, meteorology, agriculture, and the development of the resources of the colony generally. A sanitary commission has recently been established, which, if rightly managed, cannot fail to effect a large amount of good.

The Governor and the principal members of his government encourage all these institutions, some by taking an active part in their proceedings, all by the influence of their countenance and support.

To most of the institutions referred to, officers from India can easily gain access, and turn the leisure of their furlough, in a comparatively bracing climate, to profitable account.

Port Louis contains in addition, a well-organized and efficient municipality, judicial, ecclesiastical, scholastic, prison, and medical establishments, with a chamber of commerce, an immigration office, an observatory, and in fact all the means and appliances of efficient domestic government, required by the most modern standard of society and civilization. Few of these are particularly interesting to travellers, although all are of undoubted importance to the community for whose behoof they are established.

The present municipal regulations are grounded upon an ordinance passed in 1849, and are complete in their provisions. After providing for the proper valuation of all immoveable property for purposes of taxation, they regulate the subject of fires, one of much importance in a town containing so many wooden and combustible buildings. The Mayor, Deputy Mayor, and the eight members of the municipal corporation chosen for that purpose, with their badges and insignia of office, are required to attend, the police and the fire fatigue party of troops are placed under their orders, and a signal gun of alarm fired upon the occurrence of any conflagration. A portion of the excellent rules referred to might easily be adopted in Calcutta, and would prevent the wholesale destruction of property that now almost always occurs, when a bazar is attacked by fire. The rules for preventing the spread of contagious diseases, regulating weights and measures, and controlling the markets are all sound, suitable, sufficiently stringent without being instruments of oppression, and calculated to protect the public, without injury to the interests of any class of the community.

The rules for the exclusion of dangerous varieties of fish and crustacea, and for preventing the adulteration of food, would be very useful in Calcutta.

The ordinary minor regulations for the repression of gambling and disorder, the prevention of cruelty to animals, the removal and abatement of public nuisances, the supply and distribution of water, the proper regulation of the cemeteries, the relief of paupers, and similar matters are duly provided for.

The port regulations are very stringent, and some of them appear to me to be unnecessary and injurious restrictions upon commerce. The only circumstances that a visitor need bear in mind regarding them are, the advisability of never sailing in a ship with a foul bill of health, and of eschewing the society of immigrants on the passage.

What more nearly concerns those who have been sojourners for any time in that land of sugar and spice, are the regulations for departure from the colony. These are contained in an ordinance promulgated in 1850, and require them to publish their projected exit in the official gazette for the information of the lieges at large, and to prevent the escape of any intending Jeremy Diddler. Securities are required, penalties enacted, and every legal instrument set in action to protect the colony, and prevent its becoming the prey of the land sharks, and gentlemen of elastic conscience who occasionally favour the far East with their unwelcome society.

The government of the Mauritius is administered by a Viceroy, who is likewise Commander-in-chief, assisted by an executive, and a legislative council. The former consists of the Governor, the officer commanding the troops, the Colonial Secretary, and the Procureur and Advocate-general.

The latter is composed of official and non-official members. The official members comprise the Governor, the officer commanding the troops, the Procureur and Advocate-general, the Auditor-general, the Treasurer and Paymaster-general, the Collector of internal revenue, and the Collector of customs. The non-official members are ten in number, and selected from the community at large—members of the bar, merchants, and planters being found among them. The members of council and judges are dignified, as in India, with the title of honorable.

The Governor presides at the meetings, regulates the order of proceedings, proposes, except in extraordinary circumstances, all laws and ordinances for consideration and discussion, has a common and a casting vote in cases of equal division, and acts in general as moderator of the council.

The meetings are ordinarily held at Government House once a fortnight, and emergent or extraordinary meetings may be held on any other day that the Governor may appoint, a written notice of forty-eight hours being sent to each of the members by the Secretary. Eight members, independent of the Governor, form a quorum, and in the unavoidable absence of His Excellency, the senior member present presides.

The minutes of the preceding meeting are first read and confirmed, then communications from the Governor take precedence of all other business, after which, the order in which heads of business have been determined at the previous meeting by the President, is observed in the sequence of subjects submitted for discussion. The President is the sole judge and guardian of order—decides all disputes as to precedence of speech—has power to stop all irrelevant discussions, and in the event of contumacy to suspend the proceedings.

Amendments upon questions may be moved—complicated subjects may be divided into distinct propositions and considered seriatim—and considerable freedom of discussion is allowed, the speeches and sentiments of members being deemed a privilege, and not rendering them liable to be questioned either when in council or afterwards, regarding their views and opinions.

All drafts of ordinances, unless otherwise ordered, are, after the first reading, published in the Government Gazette. Each member of the council is furnished with a printed copy of the draft, to which, when published in the Gazette, notice is attached specifying the day on which observations upon it will be received by the Secretary.

The second reading of the draft cannot take place before the day specified in the notice, or at least ten days from the delivery of the printed copy to the members.

A publication in the Government Gazette of a draft of ordinance, by order of the Governor, with notice of delay for receiving observations, may be considered equivalent to, or a substitute for a first reading, and dispense with any subsequent publication of the same draft.

When the council, upon the proposition of the Governor, has decided that it is expedient to enact a law upon any subject, a Committee of members of the council may be appointed to prepare a draft of the contemplated law.

On the motion for the second reading of a draft of ordinance, the observations upon it are read, and the whole is submitted to discussion. Upon the motion being carried, the council consider the several provisions of the draft seriatim, or refer it to a Committee for examination and report.

On the second reading, no motion can be admitted but for its omission, amendment, or postponement, or if it contain different and distinct provisions, for a separate discussion and decision on each.

There are likewise special regulations for the re-examination, re-printing, and re-publication of drafts *after* the second reading, if any inconsistency or antagonism of one part to another is discovered.

The several articles of the draft being completed, the title and preamble are read and considered, and a day fixed for the third reading.

When the draft is presented for the third reading it is moved 'that this draft do now pass,' and then the discussion is confined to the general object and principle of the draft, which is thereupon passed or entirely rejected.

All questions are decided by a majority of votes, the Governor, in cases of equality, having a casting vote.

Written addresses are not allowed. All motions and amendments are presented in writing to the president, before being read by the secretary, by whom, if sent in time, copies are forwarded to each member of council prior to the next meeting of the council.

Upon the termination of a discussion, and the question being put by the president, each member present, beginning with the junior, gives his vote by saying 'yes' or 'no,' and no discussion is allowed while the secretary is taking the votes. Any member of the minority, may, if he wishes, record the reason of his dissent from the majority, at the close of the day's minutes in the journal of proceedings.

Members in discussion, are only allowed to speak once in the course of the same debate, with the exception of the member originating it, who is allowed the privilege of a reply. Members are, however, permitted to explain, and to speak upon the discussion of the separate articles of a draft of ordinance. Members requiring additional information upon subjects under discussion, can move in council for the same, or apply to the colonial secretary for it.

The same standing orders of the 16th of March 1846 regulate the nomination, composition, and reports of committees, with the duties they are to perform.

The colonial secretary is the executive officer of the council—reads and records all matters brought before the council—keeps a 'journal of proceedings'—and attends upon all committees, keeping an order book for the same.

Strangers are admitted to the council chamber ten at a time, by printed tickets from members. No communications verbal, written, or by signs are permitted between visitors and members, and the former are not permitted to express approbation or disapprobation, under pain of being required to withdraw. They are also obliged to withdraw at all times on the order of the president, or upon the motion of a member to that effect. Members address the chair standing, and allude to their colleagues by their official designations, or without naming them.

There is a special ordinance for regulating the police of the sittings of council to prevent interruptions, punish disturbances, or false reports of proceedings, and assign penalties for defamation or abuse of a member.

Reports of proceedings and debates are published by the local journals, and are frequently of considerable interest.

The form of government above detailed from official documents, is well suited to the circumstances of the colony, and gives the people a fair amount of representation through the non-official members, who, although nominated by the Governor, are by no means bound thereby to side with the government, or to cease to exercise independence of opinion and action. How far the people themselves are fitted to exercise the right of electing their own representatives, it is not easy to say. As in Lower Canada, the introduction of a foreign element renders it difficult to reconcile adverse interests, and to legislate so as to please all parties. There appeared to me to be rather too strong a leaning to the French interests, although for purposes of conciliation, than is altogether consistent with the maintenance of the British supremacy. While I should deprecate most strongly the remotest approach to class distinctions, or any departure from a proper amount of deference to the feelings, prejudices, and tastes of the inhabitants of foreign descent, it should never be forgotten that the colony is an appendage of the English Crown, owes entire allegiance to Queen Victoria, and has no right whatever to exhibit republican or any other sympathies opposed to the dominant nation. Such sympathizing would be very rudely and rapidly repressed in any part of the French Republic, were it attempted by the aliens living under the protection of her flag, and is a licence which no nation can be expected to grant further than is strictly consistent with the preservation of her own dignity and independence. Hence I conceive it to be a great political error that French law, the French language, or any practice or proceeding opposed to the feelings of the conquerors, should ever have been permitted. The rule of the Romans and of the French themselves shews sufficiently the view of the matter taken by great and enlightened nations. It cannot be compared to the British Empire in India, as in the Mauritius we dispossessed no ancient people with the hereditary claims of ages to the soil, and a religion and civilization of their own, both long anterior to the emancipation of Europe herself from the bondage of ignorance and superstition.

The history of the Mauritius from its early discovery by Pedro de Mascarégnas, in the beginning of the 15th century, to its occupation and subsequent abandonment by the Dutch, and its lengthened colonization and tenure by the French, down to the capture of the island in 1810 by the power in whose possession it still remains, is full of remarkable and romantic incidents.

Among the most striking of these may be mentioned the able administration of Mahé de La Bourdonnais, one of the most earnest, gifted, successful, and ill-requited governors who ever regulated the destinies of any colony in the universe; the wreck during his administration of the St. Geran which, as an episode in the charming tale of Paul and Virginia, has obtained a world-wide celebrity; the reproduction on a small scale of some of the atrocities and irregularities of the earliest French Revolution; the connection of the Mauritius with the almost fabulous account of piracy in the East; and the remarkable naval contest of which it was the theatre in the early part of the present century.

Some of the remains of the gallant fight at Grand Port are still to be seen, and are among the interesting objects connected with its history, that I fell in with on the island. The old iron guns that formed the battery on Monkey island, a curious bed of coral raised above the reef and covered with vegetation, are still there,—some guns of the same character are lying near the site of old Grand Port, and the rusty fluke of an old anchor imbedded in the sand, are also existing, relics of the past scenes of contest. Upon mentioning the circumstances on my return to an old Indian officer who was present at the capture of the Mauritius, he stated that he visited the Néréide Frigate at the time, and it was ascertained that with the exception of a small gallery near the stern, there was not a space of the extent of a foot, in the hull of the whole ship, that had not been riddled by round shot from the French batteries.

Of the present politics of the island, I shall say nothing, for although all parties are particularly unreserved in the expression of their opinions, it requires a more intimate acquaintance with the detailed history of the various subjects of discussion, than can be formed by hearsay, or without access to the archives of the state, to entitle a visitor to express any positive or trustworthy opinion regarding local matters. One fact, however, I learnt, which I may venture to record, viz: that the colony is in an unexampled state of prosperity, and possesses within itself every essential, if rightly applied, of happiness and contentment.

The official salaries of all classes of public servants in the colonies are lower than in India. The Governor receives £6000 a year; the chief judge £2000; the colonial secretary £1500; the treasurer and paymaster-general £1200; the vice-president and assistant judge of the court of appeal, the procureur, advocate-general and auditor-general £1200 each; the inspector-general of police £1000; the collector of customs £800; and the lower grades of public officers in a corresponding diminishing ratio.

The educational establishments of the Mauritius consist of the Royal College at Port Louis founded in 1791, and several district schools.

The former institution is ruled over by a rector and has a large staff of professors of classics, mathematics, English and French. It is an extensive establishment, appears to be well conducted, and has healthy and ample accommodation for boarders. Notwithstanding the general introduction of the English language in all the official proceedings of the government and courts of justice in 1847, by an order of the Queen in Council, there appears to me to be a leaning to French, as the vernacular language of the country, on the part of the majority of the inhabitants. This is natural enough on their part, but should not be permitted to interfere with the thorough prosecution of English as the paramount language in the college. The patois of the creoles of the lower classes is the most extraordinary imaginable medley of French, English, and Malgasch, with at times a dash of Hindustani and Malabar. As spoken by the Indian coolies it is the most laughable jargon, and the veriest lingual olla-podrida in the world. Some effort is now making to establish schools for the children of Immigrants, a wise, liberal, and proper proceeding in itself, but from what I heard not unlikely to be mismanaged, and conducted in a very questionable form. If it be intended to render French the chief, if not sole, medium of imparting knowledge, I do not hesitate to denounce it as a most impolitic, foolish, and even improper proceeding. It is no longer the authorized medium of official communication in the colony, would not be of the most remote use to those of the coolies who return to India, and would only tend to perpetuate a mischievous system, that cannot be too strongly deprecated in a British possession.

As the Indian Government is immediately interested in whatever relates to the treatment of the labourers sent from Hindustan, it is to be hoped that no such scheme will be permitted to be entertained. They possess the most effectual of all modes of compelling obedience to their wishes in such matters!

I am bound, however, to confess, and I do so with unmixed satisfaction, that this is the only point on which the most scrupulous could complain of, or object to the treatment of Indian Immigrants in the Mauritius.

All the laws and regulations regarding them are strictly and honestly fulfilled, to an extent that is almost injurious to their employers; they are not over-tasked, are highly paid, and every reasonable want and wish meets with attention. Their wages are regulated by contract of service, and are exclusive of rations, which ordinarily consist of 50℔s of rice, 4℔s of dholl, 4℔s of salt fish, and 1℔ of salt monthly. They are generally well-dressed, comfortably housed, and appeared happy and contented. They are, as in India, fanciful and changeable, but their great grievances when enquired into, are usually of the most childish and trifling description.

The following precis of the number of immigrant labourers engaged during the five years mentioned, with their aggregate monthly amount of wages earned, and the average rate gained by each, will fully bear out my statement.

	No. engaged.	Aggregate wages.	Average.
1846	47,733	£32,994 18 1	14*s.* 2¾
1847	49,638	34,339 10 4	13 10
1848	41,784	25,047 12 3	11 11¾
1849	45,284	25,365 0 4	11 2½
1850	48,112	28,683 7 4	11 11

A great proportion, if not the chief part of this is spent in the colony, yet a considerable amount finds its way to India, and must be useful to that country. The immediate influence of this wealth is, however, of minor importance compared with the intelligence, freedom from prejudice, knowledge of improved modes of agriculture, and habits of industry brought back by the return coolie to his benighted home. I had frequent opportunities of conversing with many of this class on my voyage back to India, and perceived that there was a shrewdness, spirit of independence, and worldly wisdom about the most intelligent of them, that would never permit them again to submit quietly to the crushing, heartless oppression, and utter selfishness of native zemindars, of whose tender mercies they had acquired a most correct and wholesome estimate.

It would be interesting, and beneficial to the cause it has so much, and so justly at heart, if the Government of the Mauritius would prepare and publish in India, a return of the amount of wealth taken out of the colony by return labourers, the number who had gone back to the island, and the number who had become settlers there, with the nature of their occupations, mode of livelihood, and social condition generally. In my wanderings I fell in with a few who had given up all hope and wish to revisit their native soil; they seemed comfortable and well to do, and spoke in high terms of the country of their adoption. The greatest ambition of an Asiatic is to become a landholder—a lord of the soil—however small the possession which owns him as master. This feeling might be taken advantage of by the local government, and settlements encouraged to a great extent on the waste lands, of which, I believe, there is a considerable area at present uncultivated and unoccupied.

Crimes of a deep dye are not very common in the colony. In the year 1847 seven coolies were tried for murder, of whom four only were convicted. I did not ascertain the history of these cases, but have reason to believe that the majority of such instances would be found to arise from jealousy—a frequent source of vengeance in India, where women are plentiful, and likely to be much aggravated where this 'teterrima causa belli' is so scarce. In the same year, in the whole possession there were only 522 cases of misdemeanour, in which there were 370 convictions, and 150 acquittals.

From a general tabular statement of condemnations before the court of assizes of Port Louis, for the seventeen years beginning with 1830, and ending with 1846, published in the Mauritius Mail, an excellent and able monthly statement of all matters of interest connected with the colony, some interesting facts may be gleaned.

The statement is for three distinct periods, that of slavery to the end of January 1835, that of apprenticeship to April 1838, and the subsequent period in which immigration commenced.

Nature of Crimes.	*Slavery.* 1830—34	*Apprenticeship.* 1835—38	*Indian immigration.* 1839—46	*Total.*
Abduction of minor, ...	1	..	..	1
Assaults, ...	5	..	..	5
Assaulting and Wounding, ...	5	..	..	5
Forgeries, ...	5	..	..	5
Arson, ...	4	8	24	36
Homicides, ...	..	4	..	4
Insurrections on Estates, ...	3	..	..	3
Murders and attempts at murder,	22	..	..	22
Manslaughter, ...	6	19	59	84
Poisoning, ...	1	..	..	1
Robberies, ...	90	171	242	503
Violence to females, ...	9	2	22	32
Coining false money, ...	4	..	..	4
			Total, ...	705

The whole population of all colours, classes, creeds, tongues, nations, ages, and sexes in 1846, was 161,089, and the total number of crimes committed in the same year 56, giving a ratio of one criminal for every 2876 $\frac{13}{56}$ individuals, which considering the very large number of coolies and stray waifs in the colony, is very creditable to the morality of the community.

The police of the island is organized upon the English plan originally introduced by Sir Robert Peel, and is, I believe, reputed to be efficient. For such purposes, however, I consider the French military system to be superior to any other for the rapid, certain, and effective manner in which it acts for the repression of disorder, and the apprehension of offenders.

My window at the hotel d'Europe was nearly opposite to the great gate of the jail, whence the prisoners condemned to work on the roads were mustered and marched off at day-break, under the escort of a military guard. The rattling of their chains, and murmur of their many-tongued voices as they were set in movement were in excellent keeping with the gloomy looking prison from which they daily emerged. The "stone jug" of Port Louis is an overgrown, unsightly building, constructed upon the principle of affording the least possible general supervision from any given point. Each department is excellent in itself, and not ill-managed, but the whole is a labyrinth of bad arrangement, such as must render it necessary to employ a larger coercive establishment than would be requisite with a little more attention to design. The work-shops, solitary cells, court-yard for exercise, bathing places and other details of interior economy, were good enough of their kind; but, on the whole, it was infinitely inferior to the model prison at Colombo in Ceylon.

The military establishments of the island consisted, at the time of my visit, of the 5th Fusiliers at Port Louis, the reserve battalion of the 12th regiment at Grand Port, one company of the Royal Artillery, and half a company of Sappers and Miners. Since that time the 12th has moved back to the Cape. It is at present a major-general's command, and has the ordinary staff establishment attached to it. Head-quarters are at Port Louis, and there are outpost detachments at all points of the island that are accessible through openings in the reefs. Some of the latter are in picturesque positions, but somewhat solitary places of penance for detached subalterns.

The barracks in Port Louis are very ill-placed in a low position at the western end of the town, with stagnant, swampy, filthy puddles and pools in their rear. They are enclosed in an extensive parade ground, and consist of two ranges of stone buildings, which seemed to me to be low in the roof, and ill-adapted for the accommodation of a large body of men. Port Louis is confessedly the hottest place in the island, and the barracks near the base of the signal mountain are in about as hot a position as could have been selected. That the troops are healthy in spite of this, and of the admitted irregularities of the British soldier, is an additional and a strong proof of the salubrity of the climate.

Mahébourg on the windward side of the island is a much prettier and more agreeable quarter.

The station is near the head of the bay of Grand Port, commands a charming prospect of mountains on the opposite side of the bay, is free from marshy and malarious soil in its vicinity, and must be altogether one of the most desirable and healthy places of residence in the colony.

The country around is most picturesque, boating and sea-bathing can be engaged in to an almost unlimited extent in the bay, it contains a hotel, not however, particularly good of its kind, and is in constant communication with the capital. The road from Port Louis to Grand Port is one of the best in the island, and although it is in many places extremely steep, is perfectly practicable for every species of conveyance. An omnibus leaves twice or three times a week, and the charge for an inside place is moderate.

Nearly half way at Eau Conlée and Curepipe—the former place twelve, the latter a little more than fourteen miles from Government house—are two excellent roadside inns, moderate in their charges. The difference of temperature between these places and the capital, is extraordinary and striking. I lived in the latter for three days in the wooden tenement of Mr. Gilbert, an original and most entertaining landlord, who had passed through many phases of life, and was full of quaint and humorous illustrations of his motley career. He was my guide to Mahébourg and the Savanne, and lightened all the disasters of a small dose of a deluge by his unconquerable good humour, and ingenious devices to delude me into the belief of a thorough drenching and repeated sticking in the most tenacious of earthly mud, being entertaining incidents of a trip in search of the beauties of nature unadorned by art. I left Eau Coulée early on the morning of what promised to be a clear, fine day, but had scarcely reached Curepipe when the heavens poured down their floods, and fairly washed us into Grand Port, my mercurial guide expatiating on the brilliant charms of the magnificent prospects scattered around in every direction, when I was unable to see a yard before my nose. The return from Mahébourg was more fortunate, and revealed the beauties which before had been veiled.

In the immediate vicinity of Eau Coulée are several interesting objects, to visit which it is an excellent starting point. At the very doors are curious natural caverns, and arches under which the river runs; and at a short distance is a singular punch-bowl excavation known as the 'Trou aux cerfs,' which some imagine to be the remains of the crater of an extinct volcano. Not very far removed is a remarkable inland lake, called 'Grande Basin,' which is situated at a high level, and lies in a basin surrounded by hills clothed with vegetation. It is reported to be of fabulous depth, and is conjectured to lead to all sorts of strange places. It most probably is formed and fed somewhat in the same manner as the great lake of Kandy, except that its bed is a natural instead of being an artificial excavation.

The physical aspect of the island generally is bold and remarkably picturesque, abounding in scenes of great natural beauty. It is quite entitled to the eulogistic strains in which it has been immortalized by St. Pierre, is a charming spot, pleasant to the eye, exhilirating to the spirits, and gratifying to almost every variety of taste for landscape.

The lover of the purely pastoral, the admirer of rocks and ravines, the sentimental seeker of shady glades, purling streams or brawling brooks, the venturesome scaler of mountains and heights, and the subterranean searcher of caverns, may all have their respective tastes fully gratified.

Many of the ravines are the very perfection of romantic retreats, covered with the most magnificent, luxuriant creepers, and exhibiting the course of the many streamlets leaping over the rocks in their road, in every possible variety of pretty and picturesque course. Those seen from the end of the shrubberries bounding the rural retreat of the Governor at Reduit, are singularly beautiful, whether seen from the Moka or Plain Wilhelms' side. Some of the water-falls also have a great local reputation, particularly the Tamarin and Chamarel falls. The latter I twice essayed in vain to reach, driven back by incessant rain; the former is much nearer to Port Louis and consequently better known and more frequented. It has not the grandeur of some of the falls in Ceylon and Reunion, yet it amply repays a visit, the scenery surrounding it being deemed by many the most beautiful in the island. The geologist and botanist will find ample room for pleasant and profitable excursions, particularly the former, for the true formation of the island is still a vexed question, and learned authorities have adopted very different conclusions regarding it. My own belief inclines to the volcanic view; but as I have nothing new to offer on the subject, I must refer the curious to the controversies of de Cossigny, Brunel, le Gentil and others who have investigated the question with more knowledge and means of arriving at a correct result than I possessed.

Like Bourbon, the Mauritius is completely surrounded by coral reefs, said to be eighty fathoms wide and ten feet above the level of the sea. The approaches to the island are through apertures in these banks, which can be distinctly traced in clear, calm weather.

The agricultural products of the Mauritius have gone through nearly as many changes as those of the sister-island in its neighbourhood. Cotton, indigo, spices, coffee, the mulberry, and sugar have all had their day, the latter prevailing at present to an extent that has nearly, if not quite, extinguished all other products. Since it became an English possession, the exportation of this staple has risen gradually from 969,264 ℔s French, in 1812, to 128,476,547 in 1849, the largest quantity yet produced, a truly wonderful result when the area of the island is considered, and it is borne in mind that a considerable portion is not susceptible of cultivation, or has been allowed to fall into decay. The present Governor has, with the most praiseworthy and benevolent motives, encouraged the re-introduction of the cultivation of the mulberry and production of silk as a means of affording occupation and subsistence to those unable to engage in any more laborious employment. Some of the cocoons which I saw at Reduit were excellent,

and from a statement recently published in the local journals it appears that 191 lbs 8 oz. of silk were produced in the eighteen months preceding February last, from 3,397 lbs 8 oz. of cocoons. This is small compared with the results of M. de Chazal, who in 1822, obtained seven hundred and fifty pounds of raw silk. The merit of the re-introduction is due to the daughter of that gentleman, and under the enlightened auspices of its existing ruler, it is still capable of becoming a very valuable source of profit to the colony, without trenching upon the province of the principal article of export.

The tea plant has been introduced, as it was once in Reunion, but I did not hear of any great measure of success attendant upon the experiment.

Among the fruits at present cultivated in the island are, several varieties of pine apple, the custard apple, alligator pear, the plantain, the seville orange, the lemon, the mangosteen, the date, the fig, the strawberry, the raspberry, the bread-fruit, the guava, the pomegranate, the leechee, the mango, the mulberry, the peach, the apple, the shaddock, the grape, the chesnut, the cashew nut, some varieties of plum, the tamarind, and several others of less importance.

Of spices there are enumerated cinnamon, ginger, cloves, nutmegs, pepper, all-spice, turmeric, betel, camphor, and grains of paradise.

The economical plants include many varieties of the sugar-cane, cocoa, coffee, cassia, sago, tobacco, tea, and vanilla.

Several grains, pulses and roots are also seen in some places, but few are produced to any great extent. The island is dependent for most of these substances on foreign sources.

Excellent vegetables are procurable at the proper seasons; they did not seem to be very abundant, but those which were to be had during the time of my stay, were good of their kind.

The above imperfect enumeration will give the visitor from India a tolerably good idea of what he may expect in this land of promise.

Plants and seeds from India are always acceptable, and those who go down in ships can easily carry a supply with them.

Living in the Mauritius is somewhat dear, and not particularly good. It is so entirely dependent on other countries for almost every description of food, that considerable fluctuation occurs in the price and supply of the commonest articles of existence. It is in all these respects, however, infinitely in advance of the interior of Ceylon, and the cooking is of a better order than that of the cinnamon island. I have heard that it is likewise very superior to the Cape in this essential particular.

There is an abundant supply of good and wholesome fish, plenty of fruit, well tasted and palatable, and a tolerably respectable show of fresh vegetables. But butcher's meat, butter, and milk are more scarce, and usually not of the same superior quality. The bread made from Cape and Australian

flour, is of fair average quality, and preserved articles with comestibles of every sort are abundant and good. The wines imported for general consumption are not particularly good, although far better than the average of the Indian markets. In some private families the wines, French and German, are superior to anything met with in Hindustan.

Invalids need stand in no fear of starvation in the Mauritius, and there can be no doubt that the establishment of steam communication by keeping the demands of the Colony constantly known, will regulate the supply, and render it, in future, much less subject to fluctuation than it has been heretofore.

There is a good table d'Hôte at both the hotels d'Europe and Masse, and from the latter, dinners can be obtained by those who prefer living at home in lodgings of their own. The greatest want of the colony is servants, and these it is nearly impossible to obtain at any cost.

Those in India who have old and trustworthy attendants should take them with them, paying them at the current rate of wages in the island, which is more than double that of this country. Madrasees and Cingalese are preferable to the servants of Northern India. They are less given to prejudices of caste, are more generally useful, and have no objection to sea voyages. The Mauritius has now, however, become so well known as to have ceased to be a bug-bear, and little difficulty will be experienced in inducing natives to follow their masters. For ladies with families visiting the colony, it is absolutely necessary to take every species of female attendant with them. Those procurable are of an order seldom or never employed in India, have generally engrafted colonial upon native vices, and are usually more troublesome than useful, in addition to rating such service as they are capable of performing, at an unduly extravagant estimate. The Creoles of the inferior classes are little, if at all, better. The only European female servants available are soldiers' wives. They are few in number, as well as too commonly given to gin, bitters, and barrack habits to be tolerated in a quiet household.

There are doubtless exceptions to this statement as there are to every general rule; regarding the mass it conveys the conclusion which I deduced from the information gathered in many places.

There are public baths on the Chaussée of Port Louis, opposite the Company's Garden, which are open every day, and good of their kind. The two hotels also furnish hot and cold baths. The majority of private houses are not furnished with baths of any kind.

For sea bathing a strip of beach near the old salt pans, and within a short distance of the mouth of Grand River has been appropriated. Small thatched huts have been erected there for the accommodation of ladies, and as the bottom is smooth, sandy, and slopes gradually towards the reef, within which, free from any danger of the invasion of sharks or other sea monsters whose acquaintance is undesirable, this forms a sheltered and delightful spot for the most healthful of all recreations. The favourite bathing places for gentlemen are the creek at the mouth of Grand River, and a place alongside of the Tromelin causeway.

In the neighbourhood of Mahébourg I was shewn a very perilous spot for such amusements, in the most romantic of all ravines, surrounded by every attribute of the abodes of the ancient Naiads. It is an unfinished tête de pont from which the bold bathers plunge into the deep stream below, 'dark as Iser rolling rapidly,' and soon breaking over a rugged ridge of rocks. The fall was more than twenty feet, and almost equal to a leap from the Leucadian rock.

The census of 1846, as published in the local journals, gives the population of Mauritius as consisting of 107,225 males, and 53,864 females, an unusual and in some respects injurious disproportion of sexes. This included the residents and birds of passage, as well as the military force of the island.

Of the above 30,140 males and 25,331 females were classed under the head of general population, 28,142 males and 21,223 females, ex-apprentices or the remains of the old slave population, and 48,935 males, with 7,310 females, Indian population. The disproportion exists in all classes, but is greatest, and likewise of most serious consequence, among the coolies. It is needless to dwell upon the injurious influence of such a state of affairs; it is wonderful that it does not produce more crime and disorder than are known to result from it, a fact which pleads strongly for the good government of the colony.

Until the labourer is surrounded by the influences that can alone result from the possession of a home of his own, he will be restless, errant, fond of change, anxious to return to his birth-place, prone to the commission of crime, and to acquire disorderly habits, and altogether less useful than he would and could become, were this important matter better regulated than it is at present. The colonial government is not to blame for a defect which has been felt, acknowleged, and deplored, by those most interested in the welfare and prosperity of the island.

It would be worth while for some time to come, particularly as the local revenues are now in a healthy and flourishing state, to afford additional encouragement to the migration of more numerous, and a better class of females at almost any temporary sacrifice. Were this to be done, and the local authorities in India to exhibit a direct and more personal interest in the subject of immigration than can be expected from the existing system of management, the end would be one of unalloyed good to both countries. Nothing can exceed the jealous, anxious, and scrupulous care with which the government of the Mauritius watches over the interests of, and protects the Indian immigrant. If anything, he is spoilt by the almost undue amount of consideration shown to him, and I have not the slightest hesitation in recording my conviction that he is better paid, clothed, fed, and treated in every way, than in any part of India with which I am personally acquainted.

The good faith and philanthropy of the authorities of Port Louis are now so well established, and the amount of wealth and useful practical knowledge which the coolie can and does bring back to his home so well known, that any general notification from the Government of India to the labouring population of this vast over-peopled continent would, I am convinced, awaken attention and rapidly accomplish all that could be wished or desired. A simple notice in the vernacular language of the district, pointing out the pay, and other subjects connected with the condition of the immigrant, and-made known by the civil officers throughout the country, would spread the knowledge of the existence of such a means of bettering their condition, far and wide among the ryots of Hindustan. The Coles, Dhangas, Santals, and numberless other tribes of sturdy, able-bodied labourers would, in all probability, readily embark in such an enterprize in much greater numbers, than they do at present, as the promulgation of its terms and conditions by local officers known to and possessing the confidence of the people, would operate as a guarantee of its truth and trustworthiness.

The only point respecting the coolie upon which I am disposed to quarrel with the island chiefs is the proposal to teach him French, as I have already remarked. I know of no sound principle of policy, utility, or aught else that can justify or sanction such a measure, and it cannot arise from a desire to acquire a questionable species of popularity with the Creoles, a proceeding so unbecoming a British statesman, that I should not for a moment venture to entertain or promulgate it. I have lived too long in France and among the French not to feel the deepest sentiments of respect and admiration for many of their qualities as a nation second to none in some of the highest attributes of civilization; but the genius of their language and habits, their modes of thought and action, are quite unsuited for an English possession, hence I should be sorry to see their introduction encouraged by those whose first duty is to their own country.

Although, as in India, and probably from very much the same causes, the ancient system of profuse and indiscriminate hospitality has disappeared from the Mauritius, she is still a land of kindly feeling, generous sympathy, and hearty welcome to the stranger. No where are the amenities of social intercourse better understood, more unostentatiously displayed, or more in agreeable contrast to the dull monotony, stiff formality, and disagreeable class propensities of Indian society.

The following brief and accurate description of the island is taken from the War Office returns on the sickness and mortality among the troops serving in the Mauritius. It conveys a better and more correct estimate of the matters to which it refers, than any other authority I have met with, and so far as my brief personal experience warrants the expression of an opinion, it appears to be trustworthy.

"This island is of an irregular oval shape, 36 miles in length, and from 18 to 27 in breadth, with a superficial extent of nearly half a million of acres. It is situated in the Indian Ocean, about 500 miles to the eastward of Madagascar, from 70 to 80 north-east of the island of Bourbon, and lies in Lat. 20° 9′ S.; Long. 57° 28′ E.

"From whatever quarter it is approached the aspect is singularly abrupt and picturesque. The land rises rapidly from the coast to the interior, where it forms three chains of mountains from 1800 to 2800 feet in height, intersecting the country in different directions. Except towards the summit, these are generally covered with wood, and in many parts cleft into deep ravines, through which numerous rivulets find their way to the low grounds, and terminate in about twenty small rivers, by which the whole line of coast is well watered from the foot of the mountains to the sea. Though, from its mountainous and rugged character, a great part of the interior is not available for any useful purpose, yet extensive plains several leagues in circumference are to be found in the highlands, and in the valley as well as along the coast, most of the ground is well adapted either for the ordinary purposes of agriculture, or for raising any description of tropical produce. Extensive forests, still cover a considerable portion of the districts of Mahébourg, the Savanna, and Flacq, and in the centre of the island are several small lakes, but neither of these agencies seem to exert any material influence on the climate.

"The soil in many parts is exceedingly rich, consisting either of a black vegetable mould, or a bed of stiff clay of considerable depth; occasionally the clay is found mixed with iron ore and the debris of volcanic rock. In the neighbourhood of Port Louis, and generally in the immediate vicinity of the sea, there is but a scanty covering of light friable soil over a rocky surface of coralline formation. The whole coast is surrounded by reefs of coral, with the exception of a few openings through which vessels can approach the shore, and at these points the different military posts for the defence of the island have been established.

"There is a marked difference in the climate of this island in different situations, the windward side enjoying a lower temperature by several degrees than the leeward, owing to the cooling influence of the south-east breeze which prevails during most of the year. The vicinity of the mountains also exerts very considerable influence on the humidity; and great varieties of temperature are experienced, according to the different degrees of elevation attained, so that at Moka and Plains Wilhelms, in the high regions of the interior, fires are often necessary, when at Port Louis, though but two or three leagues distant, the heat is excessive. The following table shows the range of the thermometer and fall of rain at the capital:—

Months.	Temperature.			Fall of Rain.
	Average of 10 years, 1825 to 1834, inclusive.			Average of 7 years 1828 to 1834, inclusive.
	Maximum.	Medium.	Minimum.	Inches.
January,	88°	83°	78°	6.14
February,	88	83½	78½	5.53
March,	87	83	78½	9.55
April,	85	80½	76	6.86
May,	83	78	73	3.49
June,	82	74½	71	.78
July,	79	74½	70	1.37
August,	78	74	70	1.04
September,	80	75	71	.76
October,	84	80	72	.43
November,	84	79	74	1.48
December,	87	81	75	1.87
			Annual mean,...	39.30

"It will be observed that, so far as regards temperature, rain, physical aspects, and diversity of climate, this island exhibits a very striking resemblance to Jamaica; its latitude, too, is nearly the same, though, being to the southward of the line, the seasons are reversed, summer extending from October to April, and winter during the rest of the year. The principal rainy season is from the end of December to the beginning of April, but showers are frequent at all times, particularly in the high grounds and vicinity of the mountains.

"The prevailing winds are from south-east to south, and from north-east to north. Easterly winds are rare, and usually accompanied by heavy rain; those from the west are also by no means common, and generally broken by long calms. Hurricanes are of frequent occurrence, and create great devastation, with much loss of life, but do not appear to exercise any decided influence on the health. They principally occur in January, February and March, when, in this climate, the greatest degree of heat is combined with the greatest moisture. They have often been observed to commence about the change of the moon, but no positive connection has ever been established between their prevalence and any meteorological phenomena."

The following is the average of the observations of three subsequent years, 1846, 1847 and 1850, the two former taken by M. Bousquet, a careful and scientific observer. They are for the level of Port Louis, and consequently the heat is seven or eight degrees higher than at Moka, or the freely exposed positions of the windward aspect of the island.

	Barometer.	*Thermometer.*
January 1846,	30° 07	85° 40
1847,	30° 05	85° 40
1850,	29° 94	81° 10

A cyclone was experienced towards the latter end of the last mentioned* period, passing N. E. to S. W. but on the northward of the Mauritius, travelling from the directions referred to, and passing N. W. and W. of Bourbon. It was accompanied with much rain, and some electric phenomena.

February 1846,	29° 92	86° 75
1847,	29° 99	83° 00
1850,	29° 98	83° 30

There was a gale also in this month with are abundant down-pour of rain.*

March 1846,	30° 40	86° 50
1847,	30° 08	84° 00
1850,	29° 92	81° 40

Beautifully clear weather and gentle showers.*

April 1846,	30° 07	84° 20
1847,	30° 07	83° 57
1850,	30° 06	80° 80

A very fine month: some brilliant meteors seen.*

May 1846,	30° 10	82° 75
1847,	30° 15	78° 98
1850,	30° 12	78° 50

Weather clear and fine—very little rain, and heavy dew at night. Cool season commenced.*

June 1846,	30° 20	72° 80
1847,	30° 17	75° 60
1850,	30° 19	75° 70

* These notes of the weather refer to 1847.

A cool, pleasant month, with a moderate amount of rain, and heavy dews during those nights in which W. and N. W. winds blew.

July	1846, ...	30° 20	72° 80
	1847, ...	30° 16	74° 27
	1850, ...	30° 28	73° 33

Constantly fair with a few passing showers.

August	1846, ...	30° 26	74° 40
	1847, ...	30° 29	72° 75
	1850, ...	30° 24	73° 06

Sky rather clouded, and gentle showers almost daily.

September	1846, ...	30° 20	75° 50
	1847, ...	30° 22	74° 21
	1850, ...	30° 18	74° 00

Much rain, wind, squally and variable, and many meteors seen.

October	1846, ...	30° 14	80° 71
	1847, ...	30° 22	74° 31
	1850, ...	30° 19	77° 05

Little rain and much drought, wind variable—several meteors seen.

November	1846, ...	30° 18	82° 10
	1847, ...	30° 16	79° 03
	1850, ...	30° 17	80° 06

General drought.

December	1846, ...	30° 08	84° 40
	1847, ...	30° 08	82° 09
	1850, ...	30° 06	83° 01

Wind variable, scarcely any rain, and a gale passed at a distance.

The mean average of the barometer for 1846 was 30° 11 and of 1847, 30° 07; the mean average of the thermometer for the same years was respectively 80° 71 and 78° 80.

A hurricane occurred in February 1850, and was at its greatest height from noon to one o'clock of the day of observation.

The observations for 1850 were calculated by M. Regnaud, in the observatory of Port Louis, and are published in a tabular form, with a broken period of 1849 and 1851 in Bolton's Mauritius Almanac for the latter year. In the column of remarks it is noted that "the observations were taken at 10 P. M. daily upon the thermometer in the clock of the observatory." It is also mentioned in the same place that the average heat in the town elsewhere, was five degrees greater than in the place where the observations were mad and recorded.

The mean annual temperature of Rome is 60° 70; of Naples 61° 40; of Nice 59° 48; of Malta 67° 30; of Madeira a 64° 96; of the hill districts oı Ceylon 70° 18; of Port Jackson (N. S. W.) 62° 89; of Port Philip (N. S. W.)

59° 58; of Auckland, New Zealand 58° 43; of Ootacamund in the Neilgherries 52° 28. Taking the climate of Moka and the higher parts of the Mauritius to be seven or eight degrees lower than that of Port Louis, the mean temperature of the coolest parts of the island will be somewhat higher than that of Malta, and nearly as low as that of the hill districts of Ceylon.

The Mauritius must certainly be among the healthiest portions of the earth for Europeans, if immunity from some of the most severe and dangerous diseases of other countries be taken as an evidence of salubrity. To the drunken and depraved there is no safety in any climate, and they are as liable there as elsewhere to pay the penalty of their folly and vices, but for those who lead well-regulated lives, and are possessed of the means of living in comfort, the chances of prolonged existence are as great in the Mauritius as in the most favoured regions of the globe.

The formidable types of Indian fever are nearly unknown, and those of European character are so mild as to be less severe and fatal than in any other place in the world in which British troops are quartered. The mortality of those attacked is less than 1 per cent., and when the reckless habits of European soldiery, from whom the calculation is made, is taken into account, it is an indisputable proof of the singular healthiness of the climate, dependent in some degree also upon the absence of most of the causes of a class of disease too well and fatally known in India.

Diseases of the lungs are sufficiently frequent in occurrence, but with the exception of consumption, are neither very severe nor fatal to those who are ordinarily prudent. The mildness of the climate, the purity of the air, and the very moderate range of the thermometer satisfactorily account for this.

The difference of temperature between the windward and leeward sides of the island enables the invalid, in some measure, to choose his own climate in pulmonary affections; but it is not, on the whole, ranked so high as Madeira, Lisbon, and some parts of the south of France, as a sanitarium for those afflicted with such maladies.

Dysentery and liver disease are among the most formidable complaints of the colony, but, so far as I could learn, they are more justly attributable to the habits of the soldiery, than to the influence of climate and exposure to elevated temperature. Officers and the white civil inhabitants, according to the war office returns, suffer "but little from them, the mortality from all causes at a corresponding period of life not being greater than what occurs among the troops from diseases of the bowels alone." Although the sea voyage from India, and the fine climate of the Mauritius will undoubtedly operate beneficially upon invalids who have suffered from the maladies referred to, in any part of Hindustan, I should strongly recommend their resorting in preference to the Australian colonies, which exercise a much more decided and marked effect in restoring health in such cases.

Cholera appears only to have visited this abode of health twice, and although it was milder in character than in almost any other place in which it has ever appeared, exhibited not a single feature of contagion in its course, and was tractable in treatment if taken in hand sufficiently early, it has left behind it a most absurd amount of dread in the minds of the Creole population. The ludicrous and unmanly degree in which this is exhibited when any ship containing, or supposed to contain this arch-fiend of Pandora's box, approaches the port, is one of the most painful exhibitions of human weakness that I have ever heard of. It seems to be useless to reason with them on the subject—they are alike proof against argument and common humanity in the matter. Invalids wishing to visit the colony should be very careful to ascertain that the ship carries a clean bill of health, or they will be subjected to the discomfort and annoyance of quarantine in one of its most repulsive and disagreeable forms.

With the exception of the brain fever of drunkards, diseases of the brain and nervous system are not more common than in the healthiest parts of Europe. Hydrophobia is said to be very frequent, but can scarcely be considered a disease of climate. Rheumatic and other complaints are infinitely less severe and frequent than in India; so that upon the whole, with the exceptions mentioned above, I consider the Mauritius to be admirably adapted to restore health from the majority of Indian diseases to which Europeans are liable, and for which change of climate is necessary.

It is, on the other hand singularly fatal, as is Reunion, to the Negro race. It does not appear to be particularly unhealthy to Indian labourers, but I have not seen sufficient data on the subject to enable me to form a definite opinion on this point.

The majority of those with whom I came in contact were robust and much more healthy and vigorous looking than they are in their own country. Out of a return batch of nearly three hundred who came up to Calcutta in the ship with me, there was only one sickly looking individual, and he was more lean and lanky than positively unhealthy.

From a statement of mortality among the Indian immigrants during the years 1845, 46 and 47, published in one of the Mauritius journals, and said to have been compiled from official documents, there appear to have died, in

	Men.	Women.	Children.
1845................	1283	127	37
1846................	797	121	45
1847................	530	75	13

The number of new immigrants in the colony on the 1st of January 1848, as given by the same authority, was 43,865 men, 7,355 women, and 3,887 children. If these numbers represent an approximation to the whole number in the island at the time, the mortality is high, and the climate not much more adapted for Asiatics than it is for Africans. But, as I have already mentioned, I should not have arrived at this conclusion from their physical aspect when seen at work on the estates, and in the absence of positive data as to the nature of the diseases to which they are liable, it would be wrong to give any decided opinion. It would be well, however, for the Government of India to call for an exact return of mortality, with its causes, from the very commencement of the introduction of Indian labourers, to set so important a question at rest.

In 1818, a M. Tiedeman discovered a mineral spring, chalybeate in character, on the heights of the Champ de Lort, adjoining the Champ de Mars. In composition and effects it was said to be fully equal to some of the Cheltenham springs.

It appears to have been neglected of late years, although its most recent analysis as given by a Dr. Watson, would shew that it is capable of being very useful in those diseases for which such remedies are suited.

If correct, his result is as follows, the quantity analysed being a quart of the chalybeate.

Carbonate of Magnesia, } ,, ,, Lime, ... }	5.50
Chloride of Sodium,	50.00
,, ,, Magnesium,	6.00
,, ,, Lime,	7.75
Sulphate of Magnesia,	32.00
,, ,, Lime,	6.25
Oxide of Iron,	.75
Silica,	1.75

Very recently at a meeting of the Mauritius Medical Society of Emulation, held on the 15th of January of the present year, a report was presented by a special commission upon the discovery of a new mineral spring at Long Mountain. It is at a distance of about two leagues and a half from Port Louis, and would seem to have been long known to the inhabitants of the place under the name of Ruisseau Rose.

It is easily accessible in carriages, and situated in a pretty and picturesque part of the country, dotted with small low hills covered with fruit and forest trees.

The source of supply is represented to be tolerably abundant, the air of the locality pure and salubrious, the situation cool and shady, and to possess all the adjuncts necessary to the formation of a sanitarium of superior character.

The properties of the water are such, as if correctly reported, will certainly render it a valuable discovery. At the spring it is said to be very limpid, without smell, and to have at first a rather pleasant taste, which subsequently becomes slightly styptic.

The temperature is 71° F. and its specific gravity 1001. When exposed to the air it retains its transparency for some time, and at the end of a few hours precipitates an ochry sediment. This was ascertained to be the bicarbonate of iron held in solution by an excess of free carbonic acid gas.

The following is its composition :—	Centigrammes.
Four thousand grammes containing oxide of iron held in solution by an excess of carbonic acid, ...	15.000
Chloride of sodium, ...	20.025
,, calcium, ...	5.020
,, magnesium, ...	5.019
Sulphate of Magnesia, ...	5.024
,, lime, ...	5.005
Carbonate of magnesia, ...	5.030
,, lime, ...	0.040
Silica, ...	5.012
Gummy matter, a trace, ...	
	82.005m.

In speaking of Salazie, I have already referred to the extreme value and efficacy of its chalybeate waters. Should subsequent observation and experience prove that the commission have made no mistake in the matter, and there is no ground for a contrary supposition, it will be an additional source of attraction and benefit of no mean magnitude to invalids from India.

CEYLON.

It would be unpardonable in a notice of the Sanitaria for invalids from Hindustan to be found in the Indian Ocean, to omit all mention of the nearest, most accessible, and best known of them all—the renowned Lanka of Hindu fable, the land of pearls and cinnamon, known to Greeks and barbarians, and celebrated for centuries in legend and romance.

Situated within the tropic of Cancer between the 5th and 10th parallels of North Latitude, a little more than a thousand miles from Calcutta, is Ceylon, one of the most fertile and beautiful islands in the whole world. Supposed at one time to have formed an integral portion of the vast continent from which it is separated by but a very brief interval, it may without much stretch of imagination be said to belong to India.

With its geography, history, statistics, and politics I have nothing to say, since all these matters have been ably discussed by many who had better means of acquiring accurate information than I possessed, and who were more fitted to do justice to such a task. My sole object is to record a few brief memoranda regarding its advantages as a resort for those in search of health, and my remarks must be brief, as there remains but little spare space for the completion of my 'rough notes.'

Regarding the means of reaching Ceylon little need be mentioned beyond the fact known to all, that the magnificent vessels of the Peninsular and Oriental Company visit the port of Galle every month, and will, ere long, establish a fortnightly communication with that place. I have now journeyed many times in those floating castles, and found them as complete and perfect in their internal economy and arrangements, as can be expected or desired. To please every taste is proverbially impossible. I have not yet seen any just or reasonable ground for complaint, and consider the steamers in question to be well adapted to carry invalids in comfort and safety to their destination.

The only changes I would recommend are, a diminution in the rates of passage money to enable persons of small means to partake of advantages now denied to them, a result that I am convinced would ultimately be profitable to the liberal company to which is now entrusted the command of the steam navigation of the eastern seas; and to abolish the supply of wines and spirits, each person paying for his own consumption, as in the case of the American Ocean Steamers.

The members of the 'eat-and-swill' family who frequent the saloons of the vessels are very numerous, and their 'grog-swig' propensities great under the existing system, which also entails the disadvantage of the disciples of Father Matthew paying for the libations of the worshippers of the rosy god. The result is neither pleasant nor profitable to the majority of passengers by the overland route, as it is somewhat facetiously denominated.

The chief defect in the construction of these fine vessels, is in the important department of ventilation, to which it is to be hoped that, in future, a larger amount of attention will be paid. With the powerful machinery at command whenever the steam is up, there can surely be no great or insuperable mechanical difficulty in forcing an abundaut supply of pure, fresh air, into every habitable space of the ship.

Galle, or Point de Galle, as it is most commonly called, is now the chief port of Ceylon, and the place of disembarkation for all travellers from India and England. It is situated in Lat. 6° 0′ 59″ N. and Long. 80° 17′ 2″ E. and possesses a pretty and safe harbour, capable of containing and sheltering vessels of the largest tonnage. The entrance to the bay is rendered somewhat difficult, particularly during the S. W. Monsoon, by sunken rocks, but these are so well known, and so easily avoided, that accidents rarely, if ever, happen. The first view of the fort, town, light-house, and surrounding hills clothed in the most dense aud luxuriant of tropical vegetation is extremely pretty and picturesque.

The landing is generally safe and easy, either in broad boats of European design and construction, or the quaint, cranky-looking native crafts, appearing as if they were scooped out of the trunk of a large tree, and protected by an unsightly, but very efficient out-rigger. The landing place is a wooden jetty, at the end of which are the custom-house and its appendages. The chief portion of the town is placed within the fort, a most unsightly Dutch structure, somewhat out of keeping with the pleasant panorama presented by the bay, yet possessing an air of substantial, matter-of-fact solidity, characteristic of the famous people to whom it owes its origin.

The entrance to the fort is through a dilapidated, doujon-ish, arched gateway, immediately in front of which is the guard house. The streets are narrow, in some places steep, and in all close, crowded, ill-ventilated, and not particularly captivating.

The hotels are doubtless convenient, but dirty and ill-supplied, with little to tempt a traveller to prolong his acquaintance with them. The boarding houses are better, and preferable for those compelled, or desirous to take up their abode in such a pent-up prison.

The ramparts are pretty, and afford an agreeable morning and evening walk.

The old Dutch houses, church, and residence for the Governor are neither ornamental nor remarkable, the only really striking object in the place being the light-house, a graceful iron structure of recent origin.

The neighbourhood of Galle is extremely pretty, particularly the green hills by which it is surrounded, some of which command extensive and delightful prospects, and are crowned by commodious and comfortable bungalows. The best is that of Dr. Garstin, on the highest hill, called *Erinboro* by an Hibernian corruption of its vernacular patronymic. It is admirably adapted as an intermediate sanitarium for invalids from India, who require sea air and a moderate change of climate, without resorting to the more decided depression of the hill stations. The bungalow itself is roomy, well constructed, and has attached to it every convenience in the shape of outhouses, with an excellent garden, and a good road, both from the fort to the hill, and from the base to the summit of the elevation. It is, I believe, for sale at a moderate price, and ought to be secured for Calcutta denizens who wish to run down for a brief stay without visiting the interior.

One of the most pleasant excursions in the neighbourhood of Galle, is to the missionary station at Baddygamma on the Gindura river. The station consists of a tolerably handsome church, with schools and residences for the missionaries attached. It is upon the summit of a lofty hill at the foot of which runs the river, and it commands one of the finest views in the island. It has been likened to the view from Richmond, but is more extensive, variegated, and the country covered with a luxuriance of graceful vegetation to be seen only in tropical regions.

The communication between Galle, Colombo, and Kandy, is by means of mail coaches, with flat roofs, open sides secured with canvas curtains, and very hard unyielding springs. The mail starts at gun-fire every morning, and reaches Colombo at 4 or 5 in the afternoon, the distance traversed being about 72 miles. The pace is good throughout, and the road excellent. For the greater part of the way it skirts along the sea-shore, lined with cocoa-nut palms, which here flourish in extreme luxuriance; in fact it appears as if all the members of this elegant oriental family had originally migrated from the low land of Ceylon, so numerous and varied are they at every step and in all directions. There are substantial, and occasionally handsome bridges over the very numerous rivers that water this fertile portion of the island. In some places, before emptying themselves into the sea, they expand into small lakes, the banks of which are picturesque from the dense and brilliant foliage that lines them to the very water's edge.

There are several rest houses, as the road-side inns are here called, along the road. They are far superior in convenience and every other respect to the dawk bungalows of India.

The best of them is said to be at Bentotte, the half-way station, where travellers breakfast. It is celebrated for oysters, which I strongly recommend every one who is not endowed with the 'dura messorum ilia' most carefully to eschew, as they are extremely unwholesome, and have little of the genuine flavour of the European variety to recommend them. The bridge at Bentotte is one of the most substantial and elegant structures on the road; a portion of it had been carried away at the time of my visit, and we crossed in a large ferry boat near the site of the old bridge.

One of the prettiest places on that line is Caltura, about 25 miles from Columbo: it has a rest-house, not much frequented, and a very extraordinary looking wooden bridge over the Kalee-Gunga, which is here exceedingly broad. This is one of the routes by Ratnapoora to Adam's Peak, a place which I regret infinitely having been unable to visit, particularly during the pilgrimage in March, when it is certainly one of the wonders of the world.

The country between Caltura and the capital is full of beauty, and improves as you advance to Pantura, the next stage, between which and Colombo, the road was dusty and disagreeable, the only object of interest being the old cinnamon gardens, which had a neglected, parched, unpoetical appearance, very different from the popular notions associated with the habitat of this fragrant substance.

Colombo is approached through an extended suburb called Colpetty, where the road is, on either hand, lined with handsome bungalows, until it opens out on the Galle face of the fort. This in my estimation is the prettiest view of the place; on it are the race course and stand, to the left the sea, and on the right the lake and Slave island, forming on the whole as agreeable a prospect as can be afforded by a city built on a level plain.

The Queen's House, public offices, barracks for the European corps and artillery, the light-house, public library, medical museum, hospitals, and in fact all structures of importance, are placed within the fort. The public buildings are mean and shabby. The only object worth seeing, as far as beauty of design or execution is concerned, is the statue of Sir Edward Barnes.

The principal hotel at Colombo, which faces the Post Office, is near the library and Queen's House, and occupies one of the best positions in the town: it is a large and tolerably well managed establishment, moderate in charges, and clean. The bed-rooms are, however, close and confined, and the general arrangements not particularly well suited for a tropical climate.

The most interesting objects at Colombo are the cinnamon gardens, the prison, probably the finest institution of the kind in the East, the library, and the rooms of the chamber of commerce. The Oriental Bank is the most imposing looking structure in the town. The lunatic asylum and pauper hospital are highly creditable institutions, both under charge of young men educated in the Calcutta Medical College. It would be difficult, in any country, to find similar establishments more skilfully and creditably managed.

Colombo is a hot, disagreeable place, at which I recommeud travellers to remain as short a time as possible. Kandy is the next point to be attained, and to it a mail coach runs daily, the fare being £ 2-10, the same as from Galle to the capital. The distance is also the same. A very small amount of luggage is allowed, all in excess of which is charged at the rate of two pence a pound weight. The first part of the road is not particularly interesting, except perhaps at the bridge of boats, which is a singular and safe structure.

A little more than half way is Ambapussa, with an excellent rest-house for breaking the fast of travellers; the up and down coaches usually meet there. The ground now begins to rise and the scenery to change in character until the Kadooganava Pass is reached, the road through which is a magnificent memorial of engineering skill, equal, if not superior, to any Roman remain of the same kind and character. The following description of the scene is taken from a small brochure published at Galle, and supposed to be written by a very grave, sober, steady, anti-poetical specimen of the genus pedagogue. "Here the path winds round the face of a mountain, so that, in some places there is a perpendicular descent from the road side of many hundred feet. Fearful as the way is on the one side, it seems equally so on the other, as the towering hills on your left seem to threaten every instant to fall and crush you in their ruins. The enormous trees with stems bare of branches to the height of fifty or sixty feet, are sometimes beautifully festooned with jungle creepers. The higher you ascend the grander the view becomes, until about the middle of the pass where the scene may be viewed in all its enchanting splendour. Impetuous mountain streams rush flowing o'er the rocky beds, threatening every instant to sweep away the slender bridge on which you stand. In front the mountain descends in one unbroken line to a verdant, circular plain, enclosed on every side by hills radiating from it as from a centre. These lesser hills are backed by enormous mountains, some clothed to their summits with virgin forests, while others shoot up their bare and rugged tops above the trees. One of the hills bears a striking resemblance to Arthur's seat, near Edinburgh, and the likeness is rendered more complete from its being surmounted by the figure of a head. The whole scene is grand, and at the same time pleasing, as the woods resound with the cooing of the wild doves, their notes being sometimes interrupted by the shrill cry of the beautifully-plumed wood-pecker, or the clear, starting whistle of some large hawk."

The above, far from being exaggerated, gives a very faint idea of the beauty and grandeur of the scene, of which it is quite impossible to convey any clear or accurate impression without the aid of the pencil.

At the top of the pass is a Tuscan pillar and pedestal, crowned by an unsightly urn, forming a monument to the memory of Captain Dawson of the Royal Engineers, the officer by whom the road was planned and cut—itself the proudest testimony of his skill and perseverance.

Within a short distance from Kandy, which is now at hand, is a very singular bridge of Satin wood, spanning the Mahawelli Gunga, the largest of the Ceylon rivers. It is nearly as much aslant as the leaning tower of Pisa, yet seems tolerably firm and steady. There was little water in the bed of the stream, when I crossed it in February and March, but when full, I can imagine it to be a very grand, roaring, irresistible cataract. It has once or twice, I was told, risen very nearly to the level of the bridge.

A little beyond the Peradenia Bridge is the botanical garden bearing the same name, covering a large space of ground, and kept in excellent order.

It contains many rare and beautiful specimens of the singularly varied vegetation of this prolific island, and is well deserving of more than a single visit. Most of the plants are identified and labelled, a great convenience to all who visit such places.

The approach to Kandy from this side is certainly pretty and pleasing, although, with the exception of the Pavilion, and the old Cingalese temple and relics, there are few striking buildings in it.

The cool, refreshing atmosphere that greets the traveller as soon as the dust of the road is left behind, is singularly grateful after the heat of the lower part of the island.

Kandy the capital of the central province and country-residence of the Governor, is situated in a beautiful and fertile valley 1467 feet above the level of the sea. It is surrounded by picturesque hills in every direction, and from the elevated points in its vicinity, magnificent views of the surrounding valleys may be obtained. There are curious old native buildings in the place, which are more remarkable for historical associations, than for any claims of their own to beauty. The temple containing Budda's tooth, the old hall of audience converted into a police court, the ancient palace occupied as his private residence by the government agent, and the summer retreat on the lake, now used as a magazine, are the chief of the relics referred to.

The finest building in the place, and indeed in the whole island, which is remarkable for the meanness and insignificance of its public edifices, is the pavilion built by Sir Edward Barnes. It is well placed in a small park laid out and cultivated as a garden, and from most of the heights in its vicinity forms a picturesque object.

The house is of a brilliant white colour, and constructed somewhat in the

Anglo-oriental style of architecture, with verandahs and colonnades. Behind it is a lofty hill, along the side of which to near its summit a fine road has been scarped, broad enough for a carriage to pass up, and so easy in its gradients as to be surmounted without the smallest difficulty. It is called Lady Horton's walk, and from different points of it striking views are obtained of the Mahawelli-Gunga winding through the deep, densely wooded, magnificent Doombera valley, with the Kunckles and various other lofty hills in the distance, until on returning to the pavilion face of the hill, Kandy with its lake is seen lying in the hollow.

There are two hotels at Kandy, of which the best is Albert's Boarding House, facing the green, with the lake to its right hand side. It is an exceedingly good establishment for Bachelors, but has scanty accommodation for ladies. The public library, which is placed on the very margin of the lake, opposite the temple, is also an excellent institution, and most liberal in the bestowal of its privileges.

The principal ride and drive is around the lake, which is surrounded by a good, broad, even road, and on the lower side is protected by a massive stone parapet, with a shaded walk for foot passengers.

House rent and servants are dear at Kandy, the bazar is well supplied, jungle equipments of all kinds are procurable, and it is the central point of reunion for the planters scattered throughout the province. The branch of the Oriental Bank established there, is a very convenient institution, and like all the offshoots of that substantial corporation, is so well managed as to be of the greatest use to travellers and others who are unwilling to carry any large amount of money about the country with them.

From its height above the level of the sea, variously given as from 1467 to 1670 feet, the latter probably the most correct estimate, Kandy enjoys a corresponding diminution of temperature, but is liable to considerable local variation in the range of heat, and at the close of each monsoon is visited by frequent fogs. It rains more or less during every month of the year, the fall being heaviest at the beginning of the monsoons.

The following table of the temperature and fall of rain during the three years noted, is from the late Inspector General Henry Marshall's work on the Medical Typography of the island.

Months.	Highest Temperature.			Lowest Temperature.			Greatest variation in 24 hours.			Variations in each month on average of 3 years.	Fall of rain in inches.			Fall of rain in each month on average of 3 years.
	1817	1818	1819	1817	1818	1819	1817	1818	1819		1818	1819	1820	
January, ...	80	80	80	67	60	53	9	15	19	14	$2\frac{5}{10}$	1	10	$4\frac{5}{10}$
February,...	80	81	84	68	62	57	9	15	22	15	1	$\frac{4}{10}$	$3\frac{8}{10}$	$1\frac{7}{10}$
March, ...	80	82	87	68	61	53	11	19	17	16	$4\frac{4}{10}$	$8\frac{1}{10}$	4	$5\frac{5}{10}$
April, ...	$83\frac{1}{2}$	84	87	69	64	63	10	20	18	16	$5\frac{2}{10}$	$11\frac{7}{10}$	$7\frac{1}{10}$	8
May,...........	84	84	84	70	63	67	11	21	15	16	$\frac{8}{10}$	$6\frac{6}{10}$	$5\frac{7}{10}$	$4\frac{4}{10}$
June,..........	79	83	83	67	70	68	11	11	15	12	$6\frac{2}{10}$	$2\frac{3}{10}$	$14\frac{4}{10}$	$7\frac{6}{10}$
July,...........	78	82	81	70	66	68	7	12	12	10	$9\frac{7}{10}$	$10\frac{7}{10}$	$6\frac{5}{10}$	9
August,......	80	81	84	67	68	68	9	12	15	12	$6\frac{1}{10}$	$3\frac{5}{10}$	$4\frac{4}{10}$	$4\frac{7}{10}$
September,.	81	80	84	67	69	68	10	10	15	12	$7\frac{7}{10}$	$8\frac{2}{10}$	$5\frac{7}{10}$	$7\frac{2}{10}$
October,.....	78	78	83	68	68	65	9	9	15	11	$15\frac{4}{10}$	$6\frac{1}{10}$	$9\frac{5}{10}$	$10\frac{3}{10}$
November, .	78	80	82	67	63	61	11	11	20	14	$9\frac{8}{10}$	$7\frac{1}{10}$	$4\frac{2}{10}$	7
December,..	80	80	82	68	61	64	10	17	17	15	6	$18\frac{6}{10}$	$12\frac{5}{10}$	$12\frac{4}{10}$
							Total,.................				$74\frac{8}{10}$	$84\frac{3}{10}$	$87\frac{8}{10}$	$82\frac{3}{10}$

The sun during the day-time is occasionally oppressive, but the mornings and evenings are always cool and pleasant, from the breeze blowing through the gorges of the hills surrounding the valley.

Fever and dysentery are the most prevalent and intractable diseases to which it is liable, and are most probably chiefly due to the malaria disengaged in the lower part of the valley, which is still in some degree a swamp: the great variation of temperature is also injurious. The upper part of the valley is well drained by the lake, and the residences upon its border and along the face of the steep hill skirting it are pleasant and healthy. Upon the whole, however, I am not disposed to recommend any lengthened sojourn in Kandy to the victims of fever and hepatic disease from India.

From Kandy the next change is to a much higher level, with a very rapid rise viz. from 1676 to 6200 feet, the level of the table-land of Newera Ellia. This station is 47 miles to the south west of Kandy, the road winding for a great part of the way through a bold, mountainous tract of country, intersected by numerous streams, running through deep and picturesque vallies.

There are two modes of approach to the sanitarium, the one by an excellent road, through the stupendous pass at Ramboddc; the other by a much less accessible, but nearly as picturesque a route through the Hewahetti district and across the Maturata valley, behind the great hill that towers above the whole island.

The former is the route preferred by all sober, sedate, or sickly travellers, as it is practicable for wheel carriages, and has three excellent rest-houses, to refresh, recruit, or remain a day at, if necessary.

The latter is for a great part of the way along a mountain track, or trace as I believe it is technically termed, in which it is very difficult at times to discover any trace at all, and in other places is no easy matter to scramble up and down the stony apologies for a path. It is only practicable for bipeds and quadrupeds, yet might easily and at comparatively small cost be made more accessible.

The chief road is first to the Peradenia bridge where it branches off to the left to Gampola, passing through a flat, uninteresting country, until it reaches Gampola, where is the worst supplied rest-house I fell in with. After crossing a pretty ferry, the road begins gradually to rise, and to become more picturesque at every step, until after surmounting the steep pass of Atta baggé, the station of Pusilava is reached, which is 3000 feet above the sea, and has two rest-houses, one extremely good, clean, and well supplied.

It is in an excellent intermediate climate, well adapted for those who are afraid at once to face the very low temperature of the higher regions. Some of the finest coffee estates in the island are in the immediate vicinity of Pusilava, the road passing through the very centre of the cultivation.

A little beyond Pusilava at Helbodde, the ground still continuing to rise, the traveller comes upon the Kotmalé valley, stretched out in an almost unrivalled panorama of undulating surface, watered by a multitude of small tributary streams, rushing down the sides of the neighbouring mountains until they form a grand basin, in the centre of which they unite in a deep, rapid stream, which ultimately empties itself into the Mahawelli-gunga.

The road to Newera Ellia continues to wind round the steep sides of the mountains until it reaches Rambodde, the foot of the stupendous pass, which at once rises between three and four thousand feet. Near its lower extremity are splendid waterfalls, the sides of some of the precipitous rocks are level, their summits crowned with gigantic forest trees, and from the rest-house another, and, if possible, still more charming view of the Kotmalé valley is obtained.

I walked down the pass on my return from the Sanitarium, and found it to be nearly thirteen miles in length. The inclination of the road is said to be one foot in twelve or thirteen, and it is bounded by the hill on one side, and the deep, precipitous valleys on the other. In some places the waterfalls run under perilous looking stone causeways, without a protecting parapet, and in the season of the rains, they thunder across the road itself, rendering it a service of no slight danger and difficulty to cross them. In descending, the length of the way is shortened by small, steep foot-paths running directly from one level to another, instead of winding round the hill. The coolies carrying the baggage selected several of these, and I also tried them, but found them too precipitous and slippery to be pleasant, what I gained in distance being lost in time. I had dismounted from my pony at the head of the pass, and left him with the syce to bring after me. He attempted the same short cuts, and tumbled, pony and all, down a horrible looking chasm—wonderful to say without sustaining much damage. How they managed to scramble up again I know not. He did not make his appearance at Pusilava until three in the afternoon, when I had nearly given up all hope of seeing him again, several wayfarers having told me that my pony was lying dead at the foot of the pass.

The other road is in altogether another direction, passing along the lower border of, and behind the hills skirting the lake. I started from Kandy an hour before daybreak on Tuesday the 28th of January, 1851, by the bright light of the moon, a coolie running before me with my carpet bag on his head. For the first ten miles there was a very fair road winding up and down along the sides of the hills, with the wild stream of the Mahawelli-gunga roaring over a rocky bottom at their base.

The cool, fresh air of the morning, with the silent solitude of all around, and the ever-varying scenery, broken at intervals by the sullen and stunning roar of the stream as it forced its way over some unusually rocky obstruction, were singularly pleasing. The distant hill-tops were capped with a dense mist, which gradually cleared away as the sun rose, gilding the landscape with the most gorgeous tints.

The sides of the hills in many places were cut into terraces or ledges, like broad steps, on which paddy was sown, and plentifully watered by the mountain rills. When green they give a singularly bright velvet appearance to the sides of the mountains, contrasting beautifully with the dark foliage above and around them.

The road ends in a bridle path, which, after running through a small belt of forest, becomes rough, uneven, and at some places precipitous, until it reaches the Mahawelli-Gunga at a pretty and picturesque ford, about two feet deep at the time I crossed it.

The water was clear, cold, and sparkling, falling over a ledge of rocks bounding the ford.

On the other bank I found a sturdy galloway awaiting me. Very pleasant is the remembrance of the smart canter at which old Tom took me to my destination, scrambling up steep ascents as nimbly as a goat, descending over ugly looking rocks of all dimensions with far more ease and nonchalance than I could have managed on foot, and making a bold rush wherever the path was a gentle undulation along a hollow, or tolerably level on the slope of a high hill. On a sudden when I was in no wise expecting it, he bolted sharp round a corner, and amidst the barking of dogs and all the vocal accompaniments of a well stocked farm yard, deposited me safely at the door of the old bungalow at Rathoongodde.

Here I was first initiated into the mysteries of coffee growing, picking, and drying by Mr. Clerihew's new, ingenious, simple, and efficient process. I also witnessed the curious bug which for a time blights the plant, giving it a smoky, dingy, dark, and dead appearance, as if it had very recently emerged from the sootiest recess of an unswept London chimney. The other details of management of a well regulated coffee estate, are also to be seen there.

The park-like appearance of a portion of the scenery, with the singularly beautiful and varied effects of light and shade, rendered a ramble on the hills, through the woods, and down the dales, always and at all hours a pleasant and exhilarating occupation.

The waterfalls and water-courses with the most delightful of cold baths, and the little variation of temperature during the twenty-four hours caused an elasticity of feeling, unknown to the enervated frames of dwellers on the great plain of Hindustan.

Rathoongodde is elevated 3916 feet above the level of the sea, and appears to me to enjoy the very perfection of a mild, intermediate climate, better suited to the relaxed frame of an Indian invalid than the higher or lower ranges of the Kandian province.

The following table of meteorological observations was kept by Mr. Clerihew during 1850, and shows how very favored this fair region is by the atmospheric influences, upon which so much of health and its consequent happiness depends.

A curious phenomenon connected with the hygrometric state of the air of the place is, that no amount of damp, and the atmosphere is frequently filled with the dense, pure vapours that roll through the valley, causes mildew or mould.

1850.	*Mean height of Thermometer at sun-rise.*	*Mean height of Thermometer at noon.*	*Mean height of Thermometer at sun-set.*	*Greatest rise of Thermometer.*	*Greatest fall of Thermometer.*	*Mean height of Barometer.*	*Number of fair days.*	*Number of rainy days.*	*Number of particularly rainy days.*
January,	59.5	67.3	65.3	74°	53°	26.054	21	4	6
February,	62.2	70.1	68.0	75	59	25.879	13	2	13
March,	63.3	70.3	68.5	74	62	25.874	21	1	9
April,	64.9	70.4	68.8	74	63	25.825	12	1	17
May,	64.7	73.3	69.6	75	63	25.818	23	0	8
June,	65.1	71.7	69.1	76	63	25.804	16	8	6
July,	65.8	74.5	70.1	78	64	25.814	27	0	4
August,	65.0	75.5	69.5	85	63	25.835	16	2	13
September,	63.9	73.0	68.7	80	62	25.884	16	2	12
October,	63.1	74.6	68.6	79	60	25.844	18	0	13
November,	62.3	70.9	67.4	79	58	25.866	12	6	12
December,	59.8	61.1	65.5	72	55	25.949	19	3	9
Annual Mean,	63.3	71.06	68.26	76.5	60.4	25.8705	214	29	122

The thermometer stood above 79°7 only three times during the year. The indications of the barometer are but slightly influenced either by wind or rain.

The difference between the largest and the shortest day is about one hour.

It would naturally be supposed that the exposed lives led by the planters would be productive of much disease among them, but so far as I could learn this appeared to be the case only with those who, not liking 'soft water, take to drinking *hard.*'

The greatest drawbacks to this retired life are the scantiness and inferior nature of the supplies procurable, and in many cases the damp, comfortless, unsightly shanties in which the planters shelter themselves.

There is no good pasturage for cattle, and except in the vicinity of the large stations bread and vegetables are scarce. The ordinary beef and mutton of the island afford the most violent exercise for the teeth that I ever experienced.

This state of things might, without any very extravagant outlay, be remedied. Every thing is so entirely sacrificed to coffee, that orchards and kitchen gardens are almost universally neglected.

The good taste and scientific skill of Mr. Clerihew have rendered Rathoongodde the model estate of the island. Independent of his improved method of drying coffee, he has constructed, chiefly, if not entirely, out of materials found on the spot, the prettiest and most picturesque of Swiss cottages, of which I am able, through his kindness, to produce here the counterfeit presentment.

Added to it is every convenience for a complete farm yard with garden, orchard, and every adjunct requisite to render it a classical retreat.

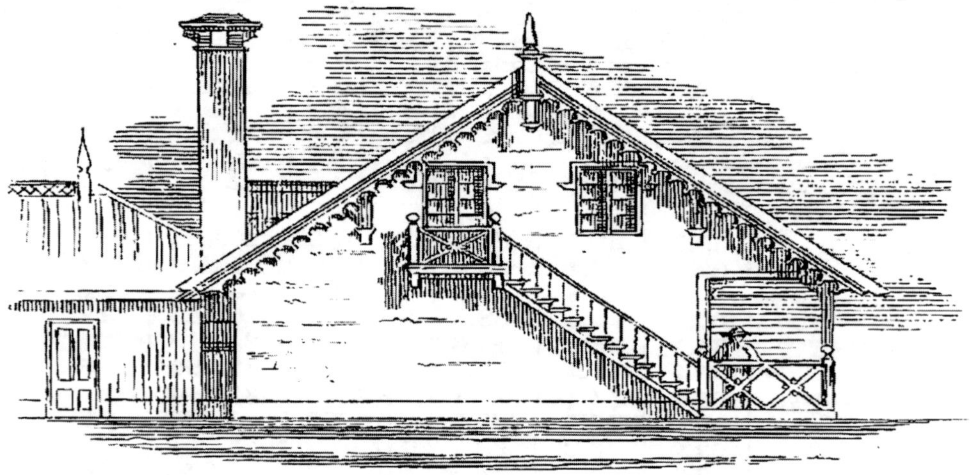

The next estate to Rathoongodde in the Maturata direction is that of Patulia, which is easy of access, and most romantically situated on the brink of a lofty precipice overhanging the valley.

From this I started at mid-day ot the 2nd of February with mine host, the very beau ideal of the most accomplished and excellent of backs-woodmen, with the tastes and pursuits of a scholar united to the hardihood and daring of a pioneer of civilization. The first part of the trip was pleasant enough, but on descending the great valley, the fierce blaze of the unshaded sun affected me to such an extent, as to cause a violent palpitation that nearly expended me before we reached our retreat. Every small elevation seemed an inaccessible height, and the very attempt to expand the chest became at last so painful, that I was obliged to lie down upon the first large stone I fell in with, and relieve my troubled spirit with a series of groans which led the astonished coolie to believe that I was about to give up the ghost.

We slept at a small planter's cabin, and started the next morning for Newera Ellia, the road for the greater part of the way being a mere elephant path, ending in the rough outline of what was subsequently intended to be a road. The forest was full of wild elephants, and we came upon the most recent traces of many of them, but in all other respects the woods were singularly still and silent. The sun never penetrates to their deep recesses, where damp, gloom, and solitude reign undisturbed. At length we emerged upon a plain, and after walking a mile or two along a path cut in a peat soil, reached our destination at one o'clock in the afternoon.

The sun was powerful, and the glare painful after the subdued light of the dark forest, but beyond being foot-sore and fatigued, I suffered no damage from the trip. To my tried and trained companion it appeared a mere morning walk, so fresh and undisturbed was he when we gained the Rest House.

Newera Ellia, the chief Sanitarium of Ceylon, was accidentally discovered by a shooting party in 1828, during the government of Sir Edward Barnes. This energetic officer visited the spot himself shortly after it was made known, was struck with its peculiar appearance and diminished temperature, and determined to convert it into a convalescent station for the sick soldiery in the Ceylon command.

It was at that time apparently uninhabited, and frequented by the natives of the surrounding country for the purpose of elk hunting. It was only approachable by elephant tracks, and a narrow path formed by the elk hunters —hence the lateness of its discovery, after the conquest and occupation of the Kandian province.

It lies on a plateau of table-land 6200 feet above the level of the sea, surrounded by lofty hills, of which the chief, Pedro Tallagalla is 8280 feet above the sea, over-topping all the other mountains around it. Adam's Peak, the renowned place of pilgrimage, long supposed to be the highest point of the island, is only 7,420 feet in elevation. Pedro is fifty miles from the sea at its nearest point—the ocean being visible from its summit on a very clear day, but this is rather rare to find, as the valleys and crests of the lower hills are constantly wreathed in the most spotless of flocculent looking mist, and the intermediate air is charged with a fine impenetrable vapour, that usually bounds the area of vision within a comparatively narrow compass. The plain, as it is not very correctly termed, is divided into two unequal portions by a low ridge of hills running from S. W. to N. East. The larger division is said to be about 2½ miles in length, and ¾ of a mile in breadth, and through it runs a river formed by numerous streamlets from the neighbouring mountains. At its lowest point it forms a species of semi-swamp, from which the valley is frequently filled with a dense fog, until the vapour is dissipated by the meridian sun. It was here proposed to excavate a lake, a proceeding that would be of infinite service to the station, and add much to its healthiness and beauty. It would not be a work of great cost or difficulty, would be a profitable source of employment to the soldiers of the detachment quartered there, and also give occupation for some time to come to the number of drunken, idle European invalids, who are now beginning to congregate at the place. It would drain the whole of the table-land, cause greater uniformity of temperature in the station, and would, in every point of view, be a work of great public utility. The river that runs through it, is one of the principal feeders of the Mahawelli Gunga.

The smaller division of the table-land is a considerable ravine, bounded by undulating hillocks, and traversed by a good road. In it are placed the barracks, officers' quarters, magistrate's cutcherry, post-office, commissariat store, and a very neat little Gothic church, the interior of which is the finest and prettiest specimen of that order, which I have fallen in with in the East.

There is still a third and smaller subdivision of the plateau, which is entirely barren and waste, with a soil of black peat. The approach to Newera Ellia from the Elephant Plains is through this barren desert, in which the red-flowered rhododendron alone appears to flourish.

The soil of Newera Ellia is said to be extremely fertile, and to be well suited for all sorts of European vegetables, cereals, and other products of temperate climates. In the gardens of the station may be seen every variety of rose, dahlia, mignionette, heart's ease, and excellent strawberries. Wild raspberries are also abundant, but the peach and the cherry do not flourish—the former never ripens, and the latter seldom blossoms. The constant rains and little variation in season seem to be prejudicial to the successful cultivation of many varieties of European plants, for which the soil and other circumstances appear to be well adapted.

There used to be, and probably are still, two Rest Houses, one of which is excellent and contains quarters for ladies, a portion of the creation for whom little provision is usually made in the island. The charges were moderate, and, considering all things, the supplies were good. The dearest thing throughout the colony is human labour, and little of this that is worth having is procurable.

During the time of my stay, with the exception of two days, the weather was pleasant, but must be somewhat trying to the weak and delicate. Early in the morning the ground was covered with crisp, sparkling hoar-frost. After sunrise the temperature rose considerably, and the direet rays of the great luminary were unpleasantly warm, while it was cool, by contrast even cold, in the shade.

The evenings were extremely chilly, and rendered a bright, blazing, cheerful wood fire a necessity. The mean annual temperature is said to be $53\frac{1}{2}^{\circ}$ F. at 6 A. M.—$63\frac{1}{2}^{\circ}$ at Noon—$60^{\circ}\frac{5}{12}$ at 6 P. M. The thermometer never rises above 70° F. in the shade, and no injury results at any season from free exposure to the sun's rays. I found it almost impossible to keep warm at night, and a plunge in one of the small natural baths excavated by the river in its course behind the rest house, was a serious trial to the nerves, yet withal, most invigorating, once the plaguy plunge had been taken.

The wet weather at Newera Ellia lasts from May to December, and sets in with the S. W. Monsoon that blows up the Bay of Bengal. It is scarcely possible to imagine anything more dreary, gloomy, and suicidal-looking than a thorough day of rain under the lee of Pedro. How the regular residents survive a prolonged continuance of it, was a puzzle to me. During the remainder of the year the sky is generally clear and cloudless, but from the chain of lofty hills by which it is surrounded, the place is never altogether free from rain, dews, and heavy mists.

From its elevation it labours under the same disadvantages as most hill climates, with their diminished atmospheric pressure, yet it is bracing, invigorating, and beneficial in removing the effects of disease contracted in the plains of Hindustan. It produces a peculiar stimulant, exhilarating effect upon the spirits, renders active exercise in the open air a species of necessity, and with the improvement of digestion, and the important functions dependent upon it for their proper exercise, exerts a most beneficial influence on the general health.

According to Dr. Beatson, who was in charge of the Sanitarium for three years, the diseases most likely to benefit by a residence at Newera Ellia are "functional derangements of the gastric, hepatic, enteritic, and nervous systems, unaccompanied by organic lesion; fevers uncomplicated with local affections; debility arising from tedious convalescence, or long residence within the tropics; and almost all the diseases of children."

Children in all circumstanees thrive there more than adults, and grow up as strong, healthy, robust, and vigorous as in Europe.

To those who have recovered health, and are able to enjoy field sports and aetive existence in the open air, Newera Ellia is an admirable spot. In its immediate vicinity elk hunting and elephant shooting, may be thoroughly enjoyed, while smaller game abound in every direction. The ascent of Pedro alone affords ample scope for constant and severe exercise, combined with a never-ending interest in the magnificent views obtained at various points towards its summit. The path is clear, and usually practicable even for ponies. By foot passengers it may be accomplished leisurely, and without much fatigue in a couple of hours, the return occupying not more than the half of that time. The summit is nearly bare, and covered by a species of cairn of rough hewn stones, with an extemporaneous flag-staff formed by the straight boughs of trees. Adam's Peak appears at hand, and the most magnificent primeval forests are seen in every direction, particularly on the side of Dimbolah. The whole sweep of the Maturata valley is scanned on a clear day, and it would be difficult, I think, to find in any part of the world anything more striking and beautiful.

The sides of Pedro are densely clothed with vegetation, and the rhododendron arboreum is found at the very summit.

Beyond the table-land, and easy of access, are the Elephant Plains, leading to the Ouda Pusilava range of hills—Wilson's Plains—the Badula district—and an extensive view of the low Bintenne country, inhabited by a wild race, little superior to the higher order of quadramana in intelligence and civilization.

The planters in every direction are kind-hearted, hospitable, and most obliging to strangers; while the wandering about among these wild hills, with the occasional difficulties to be surmounted, is the most delightful of all contrasts to the unvarying, dull, listless life of the plains of India.

I should strongly advise every traveller who intends to make any stay in the hills to purchase stout, serviceable, sure-footed ponies or mules at Kandy, where they are generally to be had at a reasonable cost. My experience in this line was not very satisfactory, as both the purchases I made came down with me, fortunately without much damage; but it was entirely my own fault, as the sacrifice of a few additional rupees would have secured me against any such catastrophe. There is no difficulty in effecting a re-sale when leaving the country, and at little loss, if the original purchase has been judicious. The wonderful instinct and certainty with which these animals scramble up and down declivities covered with mis-shapen stones of formidable dimensions, and occasionally crossed by the trunk of some prostrate giant of the forests, is surprising to those who have long been accustomed to smooth roads and a level country. Until a little experience instils confidence, it is rather a nervous matter to canter along a bridle path scarped out of the side of a huge hill, with a precipitous descent of awful depth into a roaring stream, or an impenetrable jungle at the base, the sure receptacle of the unlucky wight who makes a false step. The long, smooth, lemon grass that covers the patnas—as the naked ridges are called—frequently cover large masses of rock that render the path nearly impracticable. I remember in one place, near St. Margaret's, the planters with whom I was journeying dismounted, and sent their ponies on ahead at a dangerous spot where one of them had a short time previously nearly lost his life. As soon as we dismounted, I was compelled to become my own porter, and carry the carpet bag which until then had been borne by the horse-keeper. While toiling along under the unaccustomed burthen, I suddenly stumbled against one of these hidden rocks, and fairly rolled down the side of the hill, carrying away one or two ants' nests, full of horrid looking inhabitants nearly as long as an ordinary sized wasp. I was brought up suddenly near the foot of the hill by the trunk of a rhododendron, and found myself, in an immeasurably short space of time, seated disconsolately upon the unlucky carpet bag. The whole disaster was so sudden and noiseless, that my companions did not perceive my absence until my fall, like Phaeton's, had been accomplished. It took nearly an hour of most fatiguing exertion to recover the ground lost in two or three minutes.

The greatest annoyance attendant upon wandering in the Ceylon woods, is the presence, in countless myriads, of a most active, persevering, and penetrating land leech. I never made the acquaintance of such determined, ferocious, sanguinary monsters, inferior only to the polar variety of mosquitoe, fabled by arctic travellers to be able to bite through the sole of a boot.

In a quiescent state, these plagues are small, brown, and not unlike a juvenile specimen of the ordinary medicinal variety, but in sprightliness, activity, and determined hostility to man and animals, they are far beyond their civilized prototypes. They hop along the ground like grasshoppers, or suspend themselves from leaves and branches of trees, to assault at all points the red-blooded objects of their animosity. They can stretch themselves out nearly as fine as a hair or a thread to wriggle through the meshes of a stocking, or a woollen garment, and need no coaxing with "sugar, and spice, and all that's nice" to induce them to bite in the right place. The most effectual protection against them is the leech gaiter worn by planters, and the best means of dissolving their unholy alliance with the skin, is to touch them with brandy, salt, lime juice, acids generally, or earth oil. It is not advisable to dislodge them forcibly, as they are then apt to cause irritable wounds, which in persons of bad constitution may degenerate into formidable ulcers, causing destruction both of life and limb. They delight in damp, grassy, jungly situations, but eschew the cold tops of the higher mountains. Pedro and Newera Ellia are fortunately beyond the range of their incursions.

Ceylon abounds in most of the annoyances of tropical climates. Snakes, centipedes, ants of infinite variety and huge dimensions, with the worst and most destructive of them all, the white ant, cockroaches, mosquitoes, mis-shapen spiders, ticks, scorpions, et id genus omne of domestic monster are found in myriads.

The botany, geology, and natural history of this famous island are most interesting and will afford a perpetual source of amusement and occupation to those given to such pursuits. They are beyond the province of my very brief sketch, yet will forcibly strike all who wander through this land of many names and ancient historical associations.

NOTE ON INDIAN LABOURERS IN REUNION.

Since my return to Bengal, I have seen occasional statements in the public prints respecting the condition of Indian coolies in the island of Reunion, which led me to believe that very erroneous opinions are generally entertained upon the subject. These are not only unjust towards the French authorities, but are calculated to create a strong prejudice against facilities being afforded to the free exportation of a larger portion of the vast surplus population of Hindustan, to an interesting colony, in which their labour is much required, and where the results of their introduction must as certainly be of great benefit to themselves.

Be that, however, as it may, it appears to me to be wrong to permit any unjust suspicions to pervade the public mind, which I am able from personal observation to remove. Although I made no attempt to acquire political information in the island of Reunion, I did not deem it a breach of hospitality to note the condition of the Indian labourers whenever they fell in my way. Most persons with whom I conversed were free and unreserved in their communications, and to one of them I am indebted for copies of several of the Government ordinances regarding the immigrants. Indeed there was nothing to conceal, or regarding which the authorities could not have courted the strictest enquiry, were any inquisition necessary.

The climate of Bourbon, although probably one of the finest and most healthy in the whole world for Europeans, is extremely prejudicial to the Negro race. This, combined with their confirmed and inveterate habits of drunkenness and profligacy, when in a state of slavery, caused the French authorities many years since to turn their attention to India and China for the future supply of labour. The entire extinction of the African population was regarded by many as a certain result of the lapse of time, and the utmost anxiety was felt, lest the Colony should thus be entirely ruined, and rendered utterly useless, if not a burthen, to the mother-country, except as a Sanitarium for the unhealthy stations in Madagascar.

A few Indian servants and Chinese must have found their way to Bourbon, in vessels trading to and from Asia, very many years ago, and provision was early made for their proper treatment, as well as for their deportation in the event of their becoming dangerous, useless, or a burthen to the Colony.

I have not been able to learn the precise period at which the importation of coolies from the Coromandel coast regularly commenced. I believe that it was shortly after the publication of an able and very elaborate statistical report furnished to the Government of Charles the Xth, by a Mons. Thomas, and published in Paris in 1826. In this work was pointed out, and proved by elaborate calculations extending over a series of years, the rapid decadence of the slave population, and the ruinous effects produced by it on a country of which not more than a fifth part of the soil had ever been brought under cultivation, in its most prosperous periods.

In July 1829, in the Bulletin des Acts administratifs de L' Ile Bourbon appeared an Act relative to Indian and Chinese labourers, or other individuals of the free population of Asia.

In the preamble to the act, reference is made to a royal ordinance of August 21st, 1825, and to a local act of the 18th January 1826, the latter showing the terms on which Indian servants under personal engagement to an inhabitant, may obtain a limited permit (of residence) their masters being compelled to enter on the police register an engagement to furnish the funds to cover the expenses which the removal of their servants from the Colony might occasion. It also alludes to the authority for removing dangerous persons from the Colony, and for preventing those without the means of existence, and without a guarantee for following some profession or engaging in some lucrative occupation, gaining admission to it.

This act contained the following provisions, viz. :—

Compelling all persons residing in Bourbon who brought Indian, Chinese, or other free persons from Asia, to produce their contract or engagement with them, before a Commission appointed by the act in question.

Ruling that all such labourers and their families should be maintained by their employers and that their daily food should consist of,

80* décagrammes of rice.

12 décagrammes of dried legumes or salt fish.

And 15† grammes of salt when supplied with fresh vegetables, or an equivalent amount of other nutritious substances.

A change of diet could only be effected, by proof being afforded to the Commission of the consent of the labourers, upon being made acquainted with the reason or necessity for a departure from the first mentioned scale.

The head of the family was never to receive lower wages than ten francs a month.

Every employer of Asiatic labourers was bound to provide for their medical attendance in sickness, the maintenance of the infirm, and the means of sending them back to their native country, and to make certain specified deductions from their wages to accomplish those objects.

No deductions from wages were allowed to be made on account of the cost of the transport of the labourers to the Colony.

The Commission was to sit at St. Denis, and to consist of four landed proprietors or merchants, nominated by the Government, and of the Government Notary.

A 'Commissaire de 'l'Administration' intended to be equivalent, I imagine, to our Protector of Immigrants, was also nominated from among the public functionaries of the Colony.

* The décagramme is equivalent to not quite 154 ½ grains Avoirdupois.

† The gramme is equal to nearly 15½ English grains.

All the offices were honorary.

The Commission chose its own President and Vice-president, and named its own Secretary, as well as fixed the amount of his salary.

Three formed a quorum for business.

The 'Commissaire de l'Administration' was charged with the execution of the provisions of the decree, and was the active officer of the commission, assisting at their deliberations when he deemed it necessary, and offering his advice upon all points considered of public interest, &c.

He reported to the Director General of the Interior his representations and remarks.

The Secretary kept a general register of the labourers, in which all matters regarding them and their families were recorded.

The Secretary reported immediately on its occurrence to the President, or in his absence to the Vice-president, every case that required consideration.

The ordinary meetings of the Commission were held on the 20th of each month:—the President or Vice-president could summon extraordinary meetings whenever necessary.

The Commission corresponded through their President with the Director General of the Interior, or any other public functionary with whom it was necessary to communicate.

The Commission were to ascertain if the contract were strictly legal, and if the landholder who entered into the engagement were in a position to fulfil its conditions.

When the Commission found a contract to be *en regle*, the President signed it, and it was presented to the Commissary of Police, who was empowered to receive the subscription allowed to provide for the return passage to India of the labourers.

After all these formalities had been complied with, the license of residence was granted by the Government.

The pay of the labourers was to be issued on the first Sunday of each month at the Mayoralty, in the presence of a municipal officer, and was registered on a pay abstract prepared beforehand by the employer. When the pay had been issued, and the abstract filled up, it was signed and authenticated by the Mayor, and transmitted to the Commission.

The Commission were to see that all assignments (legal stoppages) from the pay were regularly made, and were aided by the Government in giving such facilities as depended upon it for the accomplishment of this object.

Mutual consent was required to cancel an engagement. The cancelment required to be submitted to the Commission and verified.

In all disputes between the contractors and the labourers, both parties had the right to submit the case to the Commission for official consideration. The Commission could in turn refer the labourer who had a plaint to make, to a court of consultation, legally constituted for the purpose of investigating such cases.

The Commission, without prejudice to the legal rights of other authorities, could propose to the Government the deportation of all labourers considered dangerous to the Colony, as well as those whose contract had been voluntarily cancelled, or who had been ill treated, or who required removal from other causes cognizable by law; particularly if the labourers did not enter into some other service, or adopt some other means of gaining a livelihood.

The Commission was empowered to nominate one or more chief interpreters to aid them in their function of supervision.

In case of need it could send these interpreters out into the districts to acquire information, or into the establishments of individuals, upon the requisition of the proprietor.

The remuneration of the Secretary, of the interpreters, and the cost of the Commission generally was to be borne by those inhabitants who engaged labourers. The amount was to be divided among them in proportion to the number of labourers in their employ at the beginning of the year. A fractional share was paid for all labourers arriving during the year.

Upon the requisition of the President, every one who presented his contract to the Commission was obliged to deposit in the Secretary's office four bonds, of which each assured the payment of the expenses of the administration at the expiration of the quarter noted on it.

The cost of the administration was published annually, and any balance of receipts over expenditure carried to the credit of the following year.

Measures were specified to ensure the fulfilment of the contract by the inhabitants, and to provide a camping ground for the labourers on their arrival in the Colony which was also to serve as a central place for the celebration of their religious festivals.

The provisions of this act were somewhat modified in 1831, by a local act dated the 16th of May of that year, appointing a special agent called a Syndic to act as the representative of the coolies, and to be an intermediate agent between them and the Commission.

The change was the result of a despatch from the Colonial (Marine) Minister of France, who also recommended that no special expenses should be entailed on the employers of Indian labourers, which might finally press upon them.

In June 1849, the Commissary General of the Republic published in the Reunion Gazette a notification upon the subject. He fixed the number of coolies to be imported annually, regulated the terms of contract for minors, who were never to be engaged without the consent of, or unless accompanied by their parents or guardians; declared that at least ten per cent. of women, and if possible a third, should accompany each batch of immigrants; determined that four persons for every five tons of actual register should be the maximum amount to be carried by each ship,—the ballast and space devoted to cargo being deducted from the tonnage—and laid down the rules and regulations for the supply of provisions, medicines, the formalities to be observed in shipping and disembarking coolies, quarantine, &c. &c.

One of the most important provisions of this Act was to levy a fine of from five to twenty francs per immigrant upon all Captains of vessels convicted of having failed to give to the labourers during their passage, the full rations to which they are legally entitled. This fine was independent of any police imprisonment, or action for damages from the parties concerned, to which they might be liable.

On the 18th of the same month of 1849, a supplementary order was published by the same officer, ruling that the four persons per five tons, including the captain and crew, were to be independent of the deduction made from the space occupied by merchandize or other matters in every part of the ship, except the hold.

Indians were likewise only to be stowed between decks, (on the gun deck) on the quarter deck or poop, and on the forecastle.

The same penalty as mentioned in the former order, was to be inflicted for any breach of the regulations.

I was told by those well acquainted with the subject, that the provisions of these acts are the measures at present in force regarding the coolies, and that all subsequent modifications have been entirely in favour of the labourers, so anxious are the authorities of the Colony to protect and encourage them.

In 1846 a crisis occurred in the affairs of the Colony. While 35,000,000* killogrammes or about 77,000,000 lbs of sugar had been produced, and the value of the exports of the island had been raised to eighteen millions of francs, yielding in customs revenue to the mother-country upon all the products of the island 16,000,000 of francs, the country was on the verge of bankruptcy from deficiency of labour.

There were then on the sea coast nearly 15,000 acres of land, fertile and productive, which had been abandoned for want of cultivators.

The number of plantations gradually ceasing to be wrought were increasing, and in the interior there was a vast extent of cultivable soil in a virgin state.

* A killogramme is equal to a very small fraction more than 2¼ lbs Avoirdupois English weight.

A strong and earnest appeal was addressed to the king, Louis Phillippe, in which the following expressions occur:

"In France men are without work, here labour wants men. Sire! our situation has become intolerable. The cost of black cultivators (slaves) exceeds 3000 francs (£ 120); in the course of a few years the price of a day's labour has risen from one franc to two francs and a half, and this frightful advance has not yet reached its maximum. From this exorbitant state, the advantageous results that would have followed the new laws regarding sugar are annihilated; bankruptcy and ruin will soon replace the legitimate profits upon which we have a right to count as the reward of our exertions.

"In these critical circumstances we appeal to the high reason of Your Majesty.

"The continents of Africa and Asia possess a numerous population living in the most extreme misery. Under wise protective measures, and guarantees for moderate wages issued by the Colonial Council, they would, as in the case of the Mauritius, yield us all the labourers we require to make up the deficiency that is daily increasing in our work-shops, from voluntary manumissions and the disproportion of the sexes.

"These strangers, after having aided in the increase of our crops, and the extension of our commercial relations with the metropolis, would carry back to their own countries some traces of our civilization, of our language, and of the habit of consuming the products of French industry. They would themselves become agents of civilization in their own country, as well as create new outlets for our national industry.

"The immigration of free labourers would thus become an eminently philanthropic work, and it is with the hope that our request dictated by imperious necessity, will be favourably received, that we venture to solicit from your Government authority to introduce them into our colony."

I have not seen the royal ordinances that followed this appeal, but from it may probably be dated the active and systematic introduction of labourers from the Coromandel coast, in supercession of the uncertain supply that previously found its way to the island.

The measures for the purpose, I have reason to believe, were completely organized as above mentioned in 1849, from which time, until recently, the importation has been carried on extensively.

The following is, as far as I have been able to ascertain, the general plan of proceeding now adopted.

The coolies are collected by a special agent at the expense of a ship-owner, and are brought before the French Authorities at Pondicherry or Karikal, by whom they are separately examined as to their transmission to Bourbon with their own free-will and consent.

The engagement which each enters into, to work in Bourbon for three, four, or five years, is entered on duplicate papers.

The conditions of salary, which vary according to the supposed quality, skill, and pretensions of the individual, with his scale of rations, &c. are all inscribed.

The act of engagement also indicates the advances which are made to the coolies before their departure, as well as the legal deductions authorized to enable them to return to India, or to subsist on the expiration of their engagement should they have been improvident or careless while in employ. These sums are deposited in the custody of the special Syndic or immigrant agent. As a general rule their wages are calculated to begin from the first fortnight of their arrival in the Colony.

The controller invariably covenants to furnish the coolies with food and medical attendance in sickness, however protracted it may be; the daily wages are, however, not paid for such periods as the labourer is unable to work.

He also covenants in the event of the coolie running away, or failing to fulfil his part of the contract from vagrancy, to deduct two days' wages for each day of absence without leave.

If a coolie is convicted by a legal tribunal for civil offences, and sentenced to fine, the amount is deducted from his savings, the proprietor of the coolie being compelled to advance the sum in anticipation, whatever may be its amount. The expense of punishing coolies is only borne by the state in criminal cases.

On board ship each coolie is allowed a certain amount of space as above stated, and he is victualled according to a fixed scale, as mentioned below.

On the 23rd of June 1849, a decree No. 46 relative to Indian Immigrants was published at Pondicherry. to give effect to the local acts of the government of Reunion, and the despatches of the Minister of Marine.

By its provisions immigration agencies were established at Pondicherry and Karikal, and the functions of the agents defined. The 'Mestrys,' or recruiting agents of Immigrants were placed under their immediate orders, with power to punish them in case of misconduct. The medical examination of coolies, and their regular registry were provided for, care was taken to ascertain if any fraud or impropriety was committed in causing them to come forward, and if they declared that they came of their own free will, a police passport was granted to them, with three months advance of pay. All the conditions of their engagements were to be carefully explained to them ; and minute directions were given for the complete inspection of the ships in which they were to be transmitted to their destination.

The age for contracting engagements was fixed at 21 years, and the 'Mestrys' were made to sign a declaration in the presence of the clerk of a Justice of the Peace, that all persons who presented themselves in the capacity of husband, father, mother, sister, brother, uncle, or any other relation of married women or minors, were really what they professed to be.

Provision was also made for the punishment of any fraud or violence committed towards the coolies in regard to their engagements.

On the 6th of July of the same year, an order, No. 117 of that date, was published at the same place, fixing the age of engagement of coolies at 18 years, declaring that the medical functions regarding them should only be discharged by surgeons of the French navy, or civil surgeons with regular diplomas, and making minor changes in some of the subsidiary provisions concerning Mestries.

On the 23rd of July 1849, order No. 120, containing more detailed provisions for the execution of the local acts of the Reunion Government, were promulgated at Pondicherry in the ordinary official Gazette.

Every coolie ship was compelled to have suitable boats in good condition, and of dimensions proportioned to the tonnage of the vessels. Three wind-sails were also to be provided in each ship.

Every such vessel was also to be furnished with the following scale of provisions, calculated for a voyage of 50 days—viz :

For each man daily,...	3*	litres	of water.
	80*	décagrammes	of rice.
	10	,,	of salt fish.
	16*	Grammes	of mantegue.
	40	Grammes	of dhal.
	10	,,	of salt.
	20	,,	of tamarinds.
	7	,,	of curry powder.
	5	,,	of onions.
	2	billets	of wood.

* The litre is equal to 1.760 pints, the décagramme to 154.340 grains, and the gramme to nearly 15½ grains.

In addition there was to be carried for the whole voyage—

1. 1600 grammes of avel (in case of bad weather) for each man.
2. 45 kilogrammes (each of 2.2048571 lbs. avoirdupois) of pepper per 100 men.
3. 20 pumpkins for every hundred men.

In provisions two children under 16 years of age were reckoned as one man; but the same supply of water was granted to all of whatever age.

A certain proportion of the water was allowed to be furnished by a distilling apparatus, to be kept in good working order.

The medicine chest was to contain for every 100 men—

Laudanum, ...	52 grammes.
Sulphuric Ether, ...	32
Ammonia, ...	16
Castor Oil, ...	500
Sulphate of Soda or Magnesia, ...	400
Liquid Sulphuret of Potassium, ...	1000
Or, Anti-psoric Ointment, ...	400
Diachylon Plaster, ...	100
Alum, ...	16
Chloride of Sodium, ...	3000
Lint, ...	30
Carded Cotton, ...	100
Ipecacuana, half in powder, ...	24
Mustard (in flour), ...	350
Sugar for Ptisans, ...	1000
Camphorated Spirits, ...	1000
Mercurial Ointment, ...	150
Liquorice, ...	350
Dressing Lint ¼ of a piece of 14 conjons.	

The exact tonnage was to be certified.

Infants under age accompanying their parents, to be furnished with clothing.

The sanitary state of the ship was to be reported daily by the Captain while in harbour.

The functions of the Health Commission were to be exercised by any medical officer with a recognized diploma.

No ship was to be allowed to depart without a special certificate of all necessary formalities having been complied with.

A few minor regulations have subsequently been promulgated, in the same spirit as, and for purposes analogous to those above-mentioned. They are not of sufficient interest or importance to need special mention.

Immediately on the arrival of a cooly ship in the Roadstead of St. Denis, its sanitary condition is enquired into before the labourers are disembarked. In the event of any contagious disorder existing on board, they are sent to perform quarantine at a lazaretto in the ravine of St. Jacques. When they are disembarked at St. Denis itself, they are sent to perform a simple quarantine in a very large establishment situated at the foot of the mountains, at a distance of about two miles from the town. There, or at the houses of certain medical officers selected by the Government, they are all vaccinated.

During this time their written contracts are presented to, and examined by the proper authorities, and made over to the Syndic.

As soon as they are released from quarantine, the Syndic identifies each of them, according to the descriptive roll furnished. The coolie is required to state his age, name, caste, his father's name, and the place of his birth ; and any particular marks of identification present in the individual are noted.

The whole of these particulars are copied from the general register into a book containing the copy of his engagement, and of the rules and laws relating to him, and this book is made over to the coolie himself to enable him at all times to know his duty and obligations, and to claim the fulfilment of all rights to which he is entitled. The labourer is compelled to carry this with him wherever he goes as a permit of residence, and species of ticket of leave, as well as to afford him protection from arrest or molestation.

The stipulated engagement entered into with the ship-owner at Pondicherry arms him with authority to transfer his right and title to the landed proprietor in Bourbon requiring labourers, the terms of cession being a matter of personal bargain between them. The transfer requires subsequently to be legalized by the Syndic, who enters it in the general register and inscribes it in the coolies' book also.

It is this circumstance, and the fluctuation in the price of labour which raises or depresses the value of the contracts, that has given rise to the erroneous impression in India of the coolies being sold as slaves.

The actual and average prices of the purchase of the contracts of different gangs of coolies are published in the local journals, without a statement of the circumstances in which the sales have been effected, because these are well known on the spot. Hence the misapprehension at a distance.

The working hours of the coolies are from six in the morning to six in the evening, with two hours interval for bathing, eating, and rest. Their food is cooked by one of their own caste, who has no other occupation.

No corporal punishment of any description is allowed to be inflicted by the landholders on the coolies. All offences of every description require to be reported to a Justice of the Peace, who can inflict punishment according to the gravity of the offence to the extent of fifteen days' imprisonment, with labour on the roads and in the public works. If they turn out incorrigible vagabonds, the ultimate punishment is transportation to the Coromandel coast.

In criminal matters they are liable to the provisions of the Code Napoleon.

My impression certainly is that they are treated with the greatest kindness and consideration by the Government ; that their punishments are lighter than those of the free Negro population for the same offences—probably because they are physically less capable of bearing up against harsh treatment—and that every means is taken to render them contented with their lot, and to induce them to settle on the island.

The number of women who accompany the coolies is about in the proportion of ten per cent. As in the Mauritius, they seemed to me to be of a very low order, and are probably seldom, if ever, the wives of the men they accompany.

I heard the number of Indian labourers in the island very variously estimated. Some numbered them as high as 30,000 others rated them lower than 20,000. Between 23 and 24,000, is I believe, not far from the actual number at present in the Colony. At least 50,000 are necessary to supply the full wants of the island.

They are somewhat an improvident set, fond of spending their wages in finery and amusements, and seldom have a spare rupee when their terms of engagement have expired. This was told to me by some of those whom I fell in and conversed with, natives of the Deccan. I frequently met them going to market in the morning, and the majority were in excellent condition. Prejudices of caste rapidly disappear, and although they talk about the dignity of their social position in their own country, religious scruples seem to interfere little with their wants and wishes as far as they are capable of gratifying them.

Many have settled in the country and become petty traders, and several are employed as servants in private families.

Although provision is made for their return to India, few avail themselves of it, so far as I could learn. Some of those with whom I conversed were undoubtedly British subjects from the Carnatic and Mysore territories, from the Deccan, and others were from the Nizam's dominions. It is probably not safe or correct to attach any importance to their own statements, as no two agreed exactly in their account of the manner of their engagements. They professed to be generally satisfied with their lot, and to be kindly treated. The only thing they complained of was the denial of the indulgence of the erratic propensities to which this class is so liable, from whimsical causes and mere love of change.

All deserters are quickly apprehended by the Gens d'Armes; a mounted police of European Dragoons, few in number, but the most efficient body of men for such purposes, that I have seen in the East. The deserters are tied together by the wrists and made to trot before the Gens d'Armes, always two in number, until they are made over to the judicial authorities. They are not otherwise harshly treated, in any way that I saw or heard.

There is a special hospital for Indian immigrants, and the native inhabitants of the island generally, where the sick receive every care and attention.

The above statement embodies the particulars that I was able to gather regarding the condition of Indian Labourers in Reunion, and I am convinced that they are much cared for, and well treated by the French authorities.

There can be no doubt, I think, that India possesses a vast surplus population more than the West India Islands, and those in the southern division of the Indian Ocean can possibly absorb as labourers, and that when carefully managed and justly governed as I know them, from personal observation, to be, both in Bourbon and the Mauritius, they are far better off than in their own homes.

They leave India full of prejudices, utterly ignorant, and as low in the scale of humanity as it is possible to imagine such beings to be.

They acquire in their transmarine experience, habits of thought and independence, a knowledge of improved means of cultivation, a taste for a higher order of amusements, a greater pride of personal appearance, and an approach to manliness of character, rarely, if ever, seen in the same class in their native villages. They are loosed from the trammels of caste, and abject submission to priestcraft which renders them so unprofitable a race at home. They are removed from the blighting influence, and extortionate exaction of native Zemindars, and other depressing agencies, and protected, almost to an injurious extent, in the exaction of their rights.

The spread of such men throughout the villages of Hindustan cannot fail to be beneficial, and, in my humble estimation, ought to be encouraged to the utmost limit of which it is susceptible.

They bring back wealth, vigour of body and such enlargement of mind as can be acquired in their sphere of life.